YOU SHOULD BE
DANCING
MY LIFE WITH THE
BEE GEES

DENNIS BRYON

HAWAI'I'S PIONEER BOTANIST

Dr. William
HILLEBRAND

His Life & Letters

URSULA H. MEIER

The publication of this book was made possible in part
by contributions from the German Benevolent Society
and John Lydgate.

Bishop Museum Press
1525 Bernice Street
Honolulu, Hawai'i 96817

ISBN: 1-58178-047-8

Front cover: *Hillebrandia sandwicensis*. Painting by Mary Grierson
for *A Hawaiian Florilegium* © 1996. Image courtesy of National
Tropical Botanic Garden, Kaua'i.

Book design by Julie Chun Design

Printed in Korea

Library of Congress Cataloging-in-Publication Data
Meier, Ursula (Ursula H.)
        The life and times of Dr. Wilhelm Hillebrand / by Ursula Meier.
        p. cm.
        Includes bibliographical references.
        ISBN 1-58178-047-8 (hardcover : alk. paper)
        1. Hillebrand, Wilhelm, 1821-1886.   2. Botanists—Germany—Biography.
        3. Physicians—Germany—Biography.   4. Botany—Hawaii—Hawaii Island.
I. Title.
QK31.H55M45 2005   580'.92—dc22   2005018221

To my husband Helmut and son Dirk,
who had to live with Hillebrand for many years.

Contents

Preface   *viii*

Acknowledgments   *x*

Chapter 1:   DECEMBER 28, 1850   1

Chapter 2:   HAMBURG, SEPTEMBER 1848   6

Chapter 3:   FROM EAST TO WEST   10

Chapter 4:   HAWAI'I   13

Chapter 5:   GETTING ESTABLISHED   17

Chapter 6:   BOTANY AND MEDICINE   23

Chapter 7:   A DREAM COME TRUE   29

Chapter 8:   RETURN TO HAWAI'I   34

Chapter 9:   HOME AGAIN IN HAWAI'I   38

Chapter 10:   THE GREAT QUAKE   41

Chapter 11:   ISLAND EXCURSIONS   45

Chapter 12:   TIME FOR DECISIONS   50

Chapter 13:   LEAVING HAWAI'I   53

Chapter 14:   RETURN TO THE FATHERLAND   56

Chapter 15:   MADEIRA   63

Chapter 16:   THE AIR OF *FREIHEIT* (FREEDOM)   66

Chapter 17:   A JOURNEY'S END   70

Appendix: Letters from Hillebrand to
Kew Gardens, 1857–1881   *74*

Bibliography   *131*

Biographical Timeline
of William (Wilhelm) Hillebrand

Medical Doctor, Scientist, and Public Servant

1821	Nov. 13, William born in Nieheim, Westphalia, Germany.
1844	Completes medical degree at Friedrich Wilhelm University, Berlin.
1844–49	Begins medical practice in Paderborn, Germany. Poor health forces Hillebrand to seek a warmer climate.
1849–50	Practices medicine briefly in Australia and the Philippines; then travels to San Francisco, where the Gold Rush is underway.
1850	Dec. 28, arrives in Honolulu aboard barque *Elizabeth*.
1851	Opens medical practice in Honolulu and partners with John Mott-Smith in a drugstore located at Hotel and Fort Streets.
1852	Nov. 16, marries Anna Post, stepdaughter of Dr. Wesley Newcomb, a prominent Honolulu physician and amateur conchologist.
1853	Acquires 13 acres of land in Nuʻuanu Valley and begins his garden. Hillebrand diagnoses first case of leprosy in the Sandwich Islands. Smallpox arrives in Honolulu; the epidemic spreads to all islands.
1856	"Report on Labour and Population" is published in *The Polynesian* and the *Pacific Commercial Advertiser*. Address to the Royal Hawaiian Agricultural Society, "The Relation Between Forestry and Agriculture," advocates planting trees in Honolulu to beautify the growing city.
1859	Appointed physician to the Royal Family.
1860	Queen's Hospital is built. Hillebrand is named chief physician with an annual salary of $1,500, a post he retains for 11 years.
1862	Participates in a scientific expedition to Mauna Kea, island of Hawaiʻi. The party discovers a Hawaiian adze quarry and brings back implements and artifacts that make local news.
1863	Appointed to Board of Health. Draws government attention to the rapidly increasing number of leprosy cases. He advocates a policy of isolation to stop the spread of the disease.

1865–66	Travels to Asia on a three-fold mission for the Kingdom of Hawaii: —to find sources of agricultural labor for sugar plantations; —to investigate latest treatments for leprosy; —to find and import beneficial plants and animals to the Islands.
1865	In fulfillment of Hillebrand's efforts, first group of Chinese agricultural laborers arrives in Honolulu.
1868	Travels to Big Island to aid victims of violent eruptions of Kīlauea Volcano. His firsthand accounts of the devastation make world news.
1871	July 3, Hillebrand leaves Hawai'i, departing for Germany via North America.
1871–72	Works with Asa Gray, Harvard University, to organize his Hawaiian botanical collections and begin writing his flora.
1872–86	Hillebrand researches and writes his *Flora of the Hawaiian Islands.*
1872–75	Hillebrand family settles at University of Heidelberg, Germany.
1876–85	Family lives in Madeira (Azores), Tenerife (Canary Islands), and Montreux, Switzerland.
1877–78	Appointed by Hawaiian government as Commissioner for Immigration to import Portuguese labor from Azores for sugar plantations.
1883	Feb. 3, "Investigation of the Contagium of Leprosy" is published in *The Pacific Commercial Advertiser,* Honolulu.
1885	Hillebrand family returns to Heidelberg, Germany.
1886	July 13, William Hillebrand dies in Heidelberg's Akademische Hospital.
1888	*Flora of the Hawaiian Islands* is published posthumously, completed by his elder son, William Francis, and a colleague, Prof. Eugen Askenasy.

Preface

TRACING THE LIFE OF A man who was born with a good portion of wanderlust in his blood has not been an easy undertaking. William Hillebrand, chief physician of Hawaiʻi's Queen's Hospital and founder of Honolulu's Foster Botanical Gardens, was such a man. When I began my research, equipped with a lot of enthusiasm and a few basic facts (some of them turning out to be wrong), I had no idea how far my "detective work" would carry me. But one intriguing question kept me going— who was this man who had left the green hills of Westphalia, Germany, in 1849 to set sail for faraway continents? My idea to look for answers at England's botanical emporium, the Royal Botanic Gardens at Kew, yielded success. In the depths of Kew's archives, part of an interesting Hillebrand correspondence had slumbered for 150 years.

Hardly decipherable, Hillebrand's time-aged, yellowed letters written to Sir William J. Hooker (director of Kew Gardens from 1841–1865) and Sir Joseph D. Hooker (director from 1865–1885) confirmed my belief that Hillebrand was a man of great foresight and intelligence. Despite his growing medical practice in Hawaiʻi, he had found the time to initiate a vigorous botanical exchange program with Kew Gardens and many other botanical gardens around the world, which had been a test of human patience and confidence. The survival rate of seeds and plants that found their way on often yearlong voyages around Cape Horn to Hawaiʻi were dismal. But the Sandwich Islands' agriculture desperately needed new impetus and Hillebrand was determined to give the Hawaiian growers their new species. His life's motto, "nil desperandum" (never despair), came in handy for these transactions. As my later research revealed, he couldn't have chosen a more adequate motto for his life in general.

Hillebrand loved the Hawaiian Islands and their people with all his heart. Here he found Anna Newcomb Post, the woman who became his wife, and here they raised their two sons, William "Willie" Francis and Henry "Harry" Thomas.

As secretary of the Royal Hawaiian Agricultural Society, Hillebrand founded the society's botanical garden in Nuʻuanu Valley. At their annual meeting in 1856, he proposed that the dusty streets of Honolulu be lined with fine shade trees to check the high winds that crossed the Pali. The beautification of Honolulu became one of the projects he never tired of. During the decades Hillebrand spent in the Islands, he introduced many useful and beautiful plants. Among these were the golden shower trees, poinciana, monkey pod, kauri pine, quinine, strychnine, cycads, several species of palms, plumeria, cinnamon, allspice, litchi, and many others. Botanical purists with the wisdom of today might scoff at these introductions, but then what would Hawai'i be without its plumeria and poinciana tree-lined streets?

For twenty years, Hillebrand divided his time among his three principle interests: his medical profession, his civic involvement, and his beloved garden. He became a close friend and personal physician of King Kamehameha V and Queen Emma.

In 1871, when his and Anna's health began to decline, Hillebrand decided to return to his country of birth, the newly united Germany. But his traveling days were far from over. A long odyssey through Europe followed, during which his concern for Hawaiian affairs never ceased. The successful initiation of a Portuguese laborers migration program to Hawai'i was one of them. Within the next few years, nearly 15,000 Portuguese settled in Hawai'i.

In July of 1886, a few days before his sudden death in Heidelberg, Hillebrand completed his botanical work, *Flora of the Hawaiian Islands*. He would never see his life's work in print.

A great man had closed his eyes forever, but his legacy—Foster Botanical Gardens, Honolulu's green oasis—lives on and gives testimony of his love for the Hawaiian Islands and its people.

Acknowledgments

MY FIRST WORDS OF GRATITUDE have to be sent "down under" to the amazing Australian network of botanists. I was fortunate to start my research on that continent. The response to one e-mail was tremendous. Information, advice, and photos flooded in. From the bottom of my heart, I thank Helen Hewson, Walter Struve, Darrell Kraehenbuehl, Dr. Bill Barker, Dr. Tom Darragh, and the late Dr. Sophie Ducker.

In England, I am especially indebted to Michelle Losse and Kate Pickard at Kew Gardens. They successfully searched the archives for Hillebrand's 150-year-old letters, the key to Hillebrand's life.

I am grateful to my friend and teacher, Erna Holyer, and her San Jose, California, writers group. These mentors—Rosemarie Niles, Annick Shinn, Louise Cate, Lois Maggio, Vada Jo Hollingsworth, Ronald Portal, Rita Freitas, Dale Tibbils, and John Keith—offered valuable criticism while cheering me on.

I would also like to thank Linda Wheeler, Reference Librarian, Hoover Institution, Stanford University, who helped me find Jane Hillebrand Thomson, Hillebrand's great-granddaughter. Meeting Jane, who shared her family history with me shortly before her death, was a highlight in my reasearch. I will never forget the hours I spent with Jane and her friend Edie Lauterbach.

On the island of O'ahu, my thanks go to my friends and mentors Lewis Walters, President of the German Hawaiian Benevolent Society, Hilly Weinstein, Judy Kearney, Dr. Niklaus Schweitzer, Charlotte and Peter Schall, and Dr. George Staples. To George, steward of Hillebrand's botanical heritage at the Bishop Museum, I owe a priceless debt of guidance, encouragement, and cheer.

To all of the above and many more, my heartfelt thanks.

one December 28, 1850

UNDER A BRILLIANT, HOT SUN, the barque *Elizabeth* eased its way into Honolulu Harbor. Before the eyes of the passengers rose the hills of the island of Oʻahu, their summits hidden in silver clouds. Two extinct volcanoes, known today as Diamond Head and Punchbowl, greeted the travelers. On the right bow, past the pounding surf, coconut groves shaded the native village of Waikīkī.

For William Hillebrand, medical doctor and botanist, an agonizing ten-day voyage came to an end. Racked by a hacking cough, he had left San Francisco's Barbary Coast, seriously doubting whether he would ever see the shores of the Sandwich Islands. When the weather turned after eight days of rough seas, and sunshine and tropical temperatures eased his cough, hope for survival returned to the young man. His full, dark hair blowing in the warm trade winds, the slender German joined his fellow passengers at the railing, cheering their arrival.

Regardless of their different social backgrounds or their reasons for coming to the shores of the Sandwich Islands, these passengers shared a common bond—they were adventurous travelers. They had crossed vast oceans and journeyed to faraway places, unlike the average citizen of the 19th century who didn't venture farther than a few miles from home. Most of those who crowded around William Hillebrand at the railing were disappointed gold diggers who hadn't struck it rich in the Sierra Nevada of California. Now they were in search of the riches of the tropical islands.

For 29-year-old Hillebrand, the arrival in Honolulu (Hawaiian for "sheltered bay") just meant another stop on his two-year journey, which had taken him from his native Germany to Australia, the Philippines, and San Francisco. While the other passengers had looked for gold, Hillebrand searched for a healthy climate for his delicate lungs. But botany, his true passion, was really the driving force in his endeavors. The desire to hunt for Mother Nature's undiscovered species had helped him forget his pulmonary disease and allowed him to endure months of hardship at sea.

On that December morning, when he carried his doctor's case and botanical collecting box ashore, he had no idea that Oʻahu was destined to be his home for the next twenty years, and that his advice and influence would beautify and enrich the islands of Hawaiʻi forever.

• • •

William was born in the small town of Nieheim, Westphalia. This Prussian province abounded in many of the attributes of fresh country living, boasting extensive green pastures, fertile farmland, and the amenities of the quaint district city of Paderborn with its court and Episcopal palace. When Franz Joseph Hillebrand, a respected judge at the Provincial Court, went to register his first son William on November 13, 1821, he vowed that this son would become a physician. Franz Joseph and his wife Louise Pauline had already buried two daughters at Nieheim's hillside graveyard. The noble science of medicine was much on their mind.

William's love for nature began at an early age. Together with his three younger brothers Heinrich, Franz, and Hermann, he spent days roaming through the fields and forests, learning the secrets of their natural history. At nearby Nikolaus Brook they caught tadpoles and collected watercress. On clear days they climbed the Holsterturm, an old watchtower, where there was a vista of the Teutoburger Forest. This dark and mysterious forest, in which the Germanic tribes defeated the invading Roman legions, fascinated the youngsters, incited their imagination, and made them long for faraway places.

Dr. William Hillebrand, Hawai'i's pioneer botanist.
AUTHOR'S COLLECTION

William was ten years old when he began his studies at the Gymnasium Theodorianum, a school founded in 860 A.D. There in the imposing sandstone building with its wrought-iron gate, 19 teachers prepared 540 students for an academic career. William was an excellent classical scholar. During his seven years at the Theodorianum, he applied himself to a rigorous curriculum, which included Latin, Greek, French, and English, in addition to math and natural science. The latter was William's favorite subject. At the school's library, among shelves of learned volumes, he spent long hours studying the botanical work, *Genera Plantarum Florae Germanicae,* a gift to the school by the king of Prussia. The influence of the book was enormous. Picture after picture brought William closer to the world of natural science, and the seed of his lifelong passion for botany began to germinate.

The Theodorianum's report of 1838–1840 lists William Hillebrand as its only student accepted for medical school at the University of Goettingen. The first step towards the realization of Judge Hillebrand's wish had been taken.

William took leave of his parents on a cold November day. From the stagecoach, he watched the hills and snow-clad forests of Westphalia pass in view. The coach entered the city of Goettingen after a rocky, three-day ride. To the tunes of the postilion's horn, William arrived in the kingdom of Hannover.

Goettingen hadn't recovered yet from King Ernest August's revocation of the Hannover constitution in 1837. Seven professors—among them William and Jacob Grimm, the famous Brothers Grimm—had issued a strong protest and were summarily dismissed. That breach of academic freedom was considered an outrage, and the reputation of the university declined. Hillebrand, as a freshman, was not affected by it. He took up lodging with the Kramer family on Zindelstrasse, not far from the university.

After three years, William Hillebrand moved on to Heidelberg, where he enrolled at the university's medical school on May 12, 1842. Songs and operettas describe the carefree student days at the quaint city of Heidelberg at the Neckar River, but for William hard work prevailed.

On November 11, 1843, he moved to Berlin and became a student of the Friedrich Wilhelm University. He chose that school wisely for his important last semesters. The school's affiliation with the famous Charité Clinic meant gaining insight into the newest discoveries of medicine.

But William's passion for botany also may have been a deciding factor. After all, one of the founders of the Berlin university was Karl Wilhelm von Humboldt, brother of Germany's famed explorer and naturalist, Alexander von Humboldt. Partly due to Alexander's influence, the university pioneered the introduction of many new disciplines. The school's botany lectures and field studies under the tutelage of professor Franz Mayen were renowned. His classes were filled with botany's rising stars, the future adventurers of the 19th century. Young, brave, and ambitious, these botanists were ready to risk their life in the discovery of new plants.

The "golden age" of botany had supposedly ended by the beginning of the 19th century, but for those who suffered from what was jokingly called "botamania disease," there was no holding back. At the Berlin university, they gathered to become lifelong friends or rivals. Hillebrand and Ferdinand Mueller, who received the title "baron" in later years for his outstanding work in Australia, formed a friendship that lasted a lifetime.

On October 10, 1844, after writing his dissertation, "De Vi Partum Movente," William received his medical degree. His father's vow was fulfilled.

•   •   •

Returning to the sleepy town of Paderborn with its 11,000 burghers after an active life in the Prussian metropolis of Berlin was disheartening. In addition, unemployment and poverty ruled Westphalia. Local newspapers ran big, stimulating ads: *Auf nach Amerika!* (Let's go to America!). Many young men followed that call; some townships even paid for the emigrants' passages to lessen the burden of unemployment payments.

Following the wishes of Judge Hillebrand, William hung up his shingle in Paderborn and began practicing medicine. He had grown into a studious-looking young man, with stern gray eyes and a prominent nose. Working at a Catholic hospital, and treating patients with pulmonary diseases who came to Paderborn's Ottilien-Mineral Spring for a cure, did not satisfy the ambitious young doctor. Nearly four years would pass before William could pack his bags. In March of 1848, the European newspapers reported "Gold Mine Found" and immediately another exodus of men left for California, the Golden West. But William had his mind set on Australia, a country not yet fully explored that promised botanical rewards, and perhaps a cure for his recently contracted pulmonary disease.

two Hamburg, September 1848

JOHANN CEASAR GODEFFROY, ONE OF the first European shipowners to expand trade into the Pacific in the early 1800s, was an ardent collector of botanical species and owned an enormous private collection. Godeffroy was the owner of one of the biggest German shipping companies. It was a well-known fact among his ships' captains that they gained points with their employer if they returned with interesting plants from faraway destinations. No wonder the "king of the South Seas" hired the passionate botanist Hillebrand as ship's doctor. He was even present when Hillebrand signed the one-page contract that told the young man in spare, direct words what was expected of him during the voyage.

After the signing, Godeffroy shook hands with Hillebrand, reminding him, "Always keep in mind, while on board the vessel, you as the ship's doctor represent me, the ship's owner. Therefore I expect your most excellent conduct."

One can easily guess what went on in the young doctor's mind. In exchange for a free passage to Australia, Hillebrand had taken on medical responsibility for the nearly 200 passengers and 60 crew members. He had never been on a ship before, his health not the best, and now he faced months ahead at sea with duties that could even be a burden on land. But perseverance had always been his strong point and the promise of Australia had loomed on the horizon long enough.

His trunk with the recommended clothing for the emigration— 6 shirts, 6 pairs of stockings, 2 flannel shirts, 2 pairs of shoes, 2 complete suits, and 1 warm cloak—was already on board. His plant hunt kit, consisting of a collecting box, a small portable press containing drying papers, a trowel, and a pocketknife, to name just a few items, had been stashed under his bunk.

At 4 A.M. on October 2, 1848, the *Godeffroy* had hardly left Hamburg Harbor when Hillebrand's work began. Several passengers showed symptoms of the dreadful disease cholera. In accordance with maritime law, the yellow flag went up immediately on the ship's mast. Quarantine was imposed, and the *Godeffroy* dropped anchor in the middle of the Elbe River.

After five days, on October 7, when no new cholera cases occurred and the dead had been removed, Hillebrand and the Hannoverian police found no other health obstacle to prevent them from setting sail. But now the winds had shifted. The *Godeffroy*, still on the river Elbe, remained anchored until October 12, when the winds became more favorable and took the ship out to sea.

The ominous beginning of the voyage didn't end here. The full-rigged ship had just passed through the English Channel and entered the Atlantic Ocean, driven on by a strong east wind that quickly grew into a violent hurricane. Waves exploded, towering high above the ship. The *Godeffroy* pitched and rolled, battered by waves foamed white by the fierce wind. Within several hours the ship lost use of its rudder. She was now out of control and at the mercy of the stormy sea. The 200 emigrants, most of them second-class passengers in the dark 'tween decks, feared that their life would end any moment. Gut-wrenching seasickness worsened their ordeal.

On the third day the wind slackened. But even with the passing of the storm, the sea remained choppy and rough. The crew attempted to build an emergency rudder, but that failed, and now the passengers fully realized what an enormous punishment their ship had taken. The *Godeffroy* drifted without direction. As Ernst Heyne, a passenger from Dresden, later described in a letter to a German newspaper:

> We drifted a full eight days in a sea alternately calm, sometimes stormy. In this manner we reached the Bay of Biscay, where we approached within about twenty miles of the coast. Now we were in danger of running aground at any moment, as the strong wind drove us towards the land. The captain had already indicated the place to where our corpses would float.

A plank and beams supplied by an English ship that came from Sidney finally saved the *Godeffroy*. The ship's crew fashioned a makeshift rudder and attached it to the stern with ropes. It was a wounded *Godeffroy* that limped back to England for repairs. On October 27, a pilot guided the ship into Plymouth Harbor. Safe ashore, some of the passengers actually kissed the ground. In Plymouth, Hillebrand was able to replenish his medical supplies.

Completely refitted, the *Godeffroy* set sail for Australia again on November 10. As if to compensate the travelers for four weeks of lost time, good winds drove the ship quickly forward. When the *Godeffroy* made Port Phillip, South Australia, on February 10, 1849, she could boast about having sailed from Plymouth to Australia in ninety-four days.

Hardly off the boat and still overwhelmed by their impressions of the new continent, Hillebrand and fellow botanists Otto Boesewetter and J. F. C. Wilhelmi, who had traveled with him from Germany, met in Ferdinand Mueller's Melbourne home. The jovial Mueller (1821–1896), pharmacist and doctor of philosophy, attracted his countrymen like a magnet. Even Mueller's enemies, and he would have many over the years, had to acknowledge that he possessed a great presence. A British knighthood and a hereditary barony from the king of Wuerttemberg in later years would stand the bearded, heavy-set Mueller well.

For William Hillebrand, his friend Mueller was the anchor in the New World. Mueller introduced him to Hans Hermann Behr (1818–1904), a German physician and botanist who had arrived two years earlier. With Behr, William would share future adventures.

On April 3, 1849, the name William Hillebrand appeared in the Medical Register of South Australia, authorizing him to practice medicine. By then, he had moved to Adelaide where he worked out of Oswald's Pharmacy. As soon as his financial needs were somewhat secured by his medical practice, he began to explore the countryside. Hillebrand enjoyed many botanical excursions to the mouth of the river Murray and Lake Alexandrina, and to the vicinity of Reedy Creek.

Two attractive shrubs named in his honor, *Phebalium hillebrandii* and *Veronica hillebrandii*, are unfortunately now rare in South Australia. Both species were described by Mueller in 1855 in *Transactions of the Philosophical Society of Victoria*. The former was described as an Eriostemon. In *Transactions*, Mueller stated, "It might be almost considered a genus distinct of both (Eristemon and Phebalium); and South Australian specimens have been under these considerations distributed with the name Hillebrandia Australiasica."

After only six months, despite his botanical success, Hillebrand was back aboard a ship on his way to the Philippines. It may have been that the Australian climate didn't agree with William's pulmonary condition, or that South Australia already had the presence of one great botanist. But then, William could always find a reason to justify his wanderlust. Although he turned his back on Australia, his friendship with Mueller had become strong and lasted a lifetime. In letters to Sir Joseph D. Hooker, director of Kew Gardens, Hillebrand often wrote about his great esteem for his friend in Australia and he thanked Sir Joseph for each favorable mention of Mueller.

Together with Hans Hermann Behr, Hillebrand set out to see more of the world. No two more diverse people could have joined for such an endeavor than the happy-go-lucky Behr and the stern, meticulous Hillebrand. Behr, despite being a serious physician and botanist, always had lived the lifestyle of a Bohemian. His long, flowing blond hair, pink cheeks, and twinkling eyes complimented this assumption. In his later life as director of the Natural Science Museum of San Francisco, he befriended Hillebrand's much younger brother-in-law, Thomas Newcomb. The two were among the founders of San Francisco's famous Bohemian Club.

three From East to West

THE PHILIPPINES, WITH ITS HUNDREDS of orchid species, mangrove swamps, and misty rainforests, constituted a botanist's dream. The many fragrant, flowering shrubs, vines, and trees fascinated Hillebrand and left an unforgettable impression.

For the young Westphalian whose experience with tree fruit had been limited to apples, pears, plums, and cherries in his native country, the abundance of mangos, papayas, litchi, and guavas were a neverending source of delight. The mangosteen became his favorite. This fruit, which has a tough, firm shell, offers five delicious edible segments once the top is removed. Hillebrand claimed to have lived off mangosteen for days during his stay in Manila. In Hawai'i, he would try to talk growers and gardeners into raising mangosteen whenever he had a chance. But the plant's weak root system was a definite problem for cultivation.

Soon after arriving in Manila, Hillebrand and Behr set up their doctor's office and living quarters near the Intramuros, the old city wall. From their house they had a magnificent view of the Pasig River that separated the city. After young Australia, the 17th-century architecture of Manila with its presidential Malacanan Palace charmed the young doctors. Soon the two Germans had a thriving practice that left them little time for their hobby. They decided to take turns exploring the Philippine Islands. But an extremely hot season with many tropical cyclones and intense humidity made travel for botanical excursions difficult. It didn't take long before Hillebrand found out that the heat and humidity aggravated his lungs. A persistent cough weakened him.

Sharing living quarters with untidy Behr was another daily challenge. For William, who considered neatness close to godliness, six months of their joint venture was enough. He realized he had chosen the wrong partner for his endeavor and packed his bags. On September 11, 1850, he boarded the old battered barque *Naumkeang* and arrived eighty days later, November 29, in San Francisco. The ship listed its cargo as "292 jars of eggs, 30 cases of segars [*sic*] (cigars), sugar, coffee and cordage. 2 Passengers: Dr. William Hillebrand and T. B. Clough."

With the rainy season in full force and 1850 an unusually wet and cold year, torrents of rain shed from the clouds, drenching the new arrivals. Shivering from cold and fever, William Hillebrand fought his way through San Francisco's muddy streets, which were covered with brush-wood, tree limbs, and planks to make them more passable. He walked past smoldering ruins of the Montgomery Street fire. Through the open doors of gambling saloons, he watched drunken miners laying their hard-earned gold upon the faro tables.

The few decent hotels filled to capacity, he had no other choice but to find himself a bunk bed in one of San Francisco's notorious boarding houses. Taking advantage of the city's rapid population increase from 25,000 to 50,000 souls, the proprietors rented out their dirty, flea-infested bunks for $8 a day. A hearty meal at one of the nearby eateries cost $5 at best.

William soon realized that staying in California would not only mean his financial ruin, but also his certain death. If the hot, sultry Philippine climate had aggravated his consumption, now he feared the consequences of California's cold winter weather for which he wasn't dressed properly. After a sleepless night on one of the hard, soiled cots of a boarding house, he dragged his ailing body back to the harbor. He later stated, "Only one thought prevailed in my mind: if I have to die, then, at least, it should happen in a warmer climate or on the way to such."

That thought helped him to overcome the following weeks. Every morning he lined up with hundreds of desperate gold diggers at the harbor, hoping to get passage to a warmer climate. Nearly four weeks passed before he finally could climb aboard a ship going to the Sandwich Islands.

four Hawai'i

ALL WAS NOT WELL IN the kingdom of Kamehameha III when William Hillebrand arrived in Honolulu, capital of the Sandwich Islands. Not even the Hawaiian sun could blaze away the fact that the booming years of 1848 and 1849 had come to an end. Sugar export was down; the whaling industry had declined. Only the demand for Hawaiian potatoes for the ever-growing population of California continued strong. Due to diseases and emigration to California, the native population of the Islands had dwindled to 84,000. The Islands' labor supply was inadequate.

But those were the least of young Dr. Hillebrand's worries when he arrived on December 28, 1850. He had lost weight. His gray woolen suit, which hadn't been warm enough for California's winter, was now much too warm for Hawai'i's climate. It hung loosely around his body. The fever and weakness that had plagued him since his departure from Manila had increased. As a medical doctor, he knew his tubercular disease had taken a turn for the worse. He prescribed for himself long hours of rest at the straw-thatched cottage of Honolulu's Eden Hotel, his first Hawaiian home. Days later, when his hacking cough left red stains on his handkerchief, he sought the advice of an American doctor.

Dr. Wesley Newcomb, friend and father-in-law of Hillebrand.
AUTHOR'S COLLECTION

It would become a fateful meeting in that small backyard hut of Dr. Wesley Newcomb's home where he practiced medicine. Hillebrand and Newcomb, who was thirteen years his senior, formed an instant friendship. Both came from similar backgrounds and had enjoyed carefree student days at prestigious universities. But what bound them so closely was that each of them shared their medical profession with a hobby. What plants were to Hillebrand, seashells were to the passionate conchologist Newcomb. His collection, sold twenty years later to Cornell University, would bring in $20,000, a rather proud sum for 1870.

The Newcomb family had arrived ten months earlier. Wesley, son of an elite family in Troy, New York, was married to Helen Wells Post, of equally good upbringing. Well-educated and of great disposition, Helen had accompanied her husband on an adventurous journey around Cape Horn without a word of complaint. A ramshackle, flea-infested, wooden house in California's bustling state capitol Benicia became their first home on the West Coast. While her husband, then a member of the Rensselaer Exploration Co., searched for investment possibilities in the Sierra Nevada Gold Country, Helen stayed in cold, muddy Benicia on the Carquinez Strait with her daughter from a previous marriage, Anna Post, and her 5-year-old son, Thomas Newcomb. Six months later, sick with ague and fever, the Newcombs gave up their dream of California gold and set sail for a warmer climate in the Sandwich Islands. The Newcombs invited Hillebrand to stay at their Hawaiian home until he regained his health.

For Helen Newcomb and 18-year-old daughter Anna, nursing the young doctor back to health became a welcome interruption in their daily routine. Preparing nourishing soups for the patient gave slender, brown-eyed Anna Post Newcomb an opportunity to show off her cooking skills.

Her ability to turn vegetables and a simple cut of beef into a delicious soup impressed William. While he recuperated under the care of the two ladies, he familiarized himself with the flora and fauna of Hawai'i. He was enchanted by the Islands right from the beginning, but he also saw Honolulu's shortcomings. After his first walks through its narrow and crooked streets, he immediately decided that this dusty place needed trees. Not just any trees, but flowering ones like plumerias, shower trees, and African tulip trees, as he had seen in the Philippines and Java.

"Watering trees costs dearly, they must be watered 6-9 months," practical Helen Newcomb objected when her guest told her of his decision.

"Then people should get a water discount rate from the city," William replied stubbornly. He was determined to change the appearance of Honolulu. The city's ramshackle grass shacks and the littered backyards had to go, or at least be hidden behind beautiful trees and bushes, he decided.

Once his health improved, he met with O'ahu's elite. His talent for establishing meaningful acquaintances soon befriended him with many of the city's leaders. Robert Crichton Wyllie, a Scottish physician and minister of foreign affairs, welcomed the young doctor and assured him that the kingdom needed qualified men like him to set up a Board of Health and a hospital. At the Newcomb house, Hillebrand was introduced to Bernice Pauahi Bishop, high chiefess and last descendant of Kamehameha the Great. The young doctor was enthralled by her beauty, intelligence, and sincerity. Bernice, who eight months earlier had married the American banker Charles R. Bishop against the will of her parents, told her friends at the Newcomb's house that she couldn't endure the idea of being revered as the heir to the throne.

Samuel Chenery Damon, influential preacher and publisher of *The Seaman's Friend,* a small popular paper sold for $2.50 at street corners, often visited the Newcomb's and their houseguest. Damon, who considered Polynesians as equals, was a strong advocate against slavery, and a man after Hillebrand's heart. That Damon also was one of the founding fathers of the Royal Hawaiian Agricultural Society endeared him even more to the young doctor. But Hillebrand's friendship with Dr. Newcomb also entrailed animosity. A long-standing feud between Newcomb and Dr. Gerrit P. Judd, King's councillor and physician, carried over to him.

At the beginning of May 1851, Hillebrand felt well enough to attend the opening of Parliament where he listened to the speech of King Kamehameha III. By then the doctor's Hawaiian language studies had progressed to such an extent that he was able to understand most of the speech without translation.

Anna Hillebrand.

On December 15,1851, Dr. and Mrs. Newcomb announced the engagement of their daughter Anna Post to Dr. William Hillebrand. Choosing Anna as his life's companion proved to be a most fortunate decision. Anna, despite her shy demeanor, had all the attributes of a true pioneer woman. She was well-known for both her diligence and resourcefulness. Together with her parents, she had endured a troublesome voyage on an overcrowded ship from New York to California, and six months of frontier life in Benicia. The Sandwich Islands were full of new challenges, too. Anna had made the transition from an offspring of a prominent, well-to-do East Coast family to that of a resourceful, practical immigrant.

A few days after the engagement, Drs. Newcomb and Hillebrand opened a joint medical office at Hopewell Place, located at the corner of Beretania and Smith Street. A year later on November 16, 1852, when the Hillebrand-Anna Post Newcomb wedding took place, William and his father-in-law were already enjoying a thriving medical practice and high esteem.

five Getting Established

HAWAIIAN FRIENDS DESCRIBED HILLEBRAND AS a quiet, sober, practical man of medium height and weight, fair complexion, gray eyes, and possessing an abundance of dark hair. They praised his intelligence and his dignified and courteous ways. His fondness of music and talent for playing the piano made him a much sought-after guest at social gatherings. But Hillebrand's hidden strength, his methodical way of thinking and his superb ability of delegating and organizing, hadn't been noticed yet. Without these traits he would never have become an extraordinary physician and a renowned botanist.

Hillebrand and his wife established their summerhouse in Nuʻuanu Valley on thirteen acres of land. They bought a high-post bedstead for $50 at a Honolulu auction, but had the rest of their furniture made of Hawaiian koa wood. Hillebrand wrote to Sir William J. Hooker, "Are you aware what a fine cabinet wood our Koa yields? To my taste it makes handsomer furniture than mahogany. Only the cabinetmakers say it is hard to work into veneer."

His home taken care of, he began to set up his garden with the help of two native gardeners. They planted trees and other flora from Moloka'i, Lāna'i, and Maui. But his botanical endeavors came to an abrupt stop on February 10, 1853, when the American merchant ship *Charles Mallory* appeared off Honolulu flying the yellow flag, signal of serious disease on board. A passenger suffering from smallpox was immediately isolated on a reef at Kahili. An improvised and controversial vaccination program under the auspices of Dr. Gerrit P. Judd began. Quarantine stations and a pest hospital were set up.

Two months later, when the citizens of Honolulu thought they had mastered the spread of the disease, two Hawaiian women fell sick at their homes in downtown Honolulu. Like a wildfire, new cases of smallpox appeared on all parts of O'ahu. Hillebrand and his fellow physicians

The smallpox epidemic hit the Hawaiian Islands in February 1853 and didn't end until October of that year. Victims of smallpox were isolated in makeshift hospitals outside the city.

OIL PAINTING BY PAUL EMMERT, 1853
COURTESY OF THE HAWAIIAN HISTORICAL SOCIETY

dying. In August, more than 4,000 cases and 1,500 deaths were reported. In October, when no more new cases of smallpox appeared, the Hillebrand–Newcomb families sighed with relief. Anna Hillebrand, who was expecting her first child, had made it through the epidemic without catching the illness.

Years ago, under her stepfather's tutelage, Anna had become a conchologist's assistant. Now she received instructions from her husband on how to take care of seedlings and properly prepare plants for drying. When Anna gave birth to their first son William Francis on December 13, 1853, and was temporarily incapacitated, Hillebrand taught his mother-in-law, Helen Newcomb, the intricacies of botanical preservation. Thus assured that the two ladies would look after his green treasures, he felt free to work long hours at his medical office, and at the Queen's Hospital where he had been named chief physician.

• • •

At meetings of the Royal Hawaiian Agricultural Society, which his father-in-law had co-founded, Hillebrand was an enthusiastic member and acted as secretary of the organization. He spoke out as a strong advocate of a botanical garden and nursery for Honolulu. Pointing out the variety of beautiful shrubs that grew in remote parts of the Islands, he suggested that they be transplanted in populated areas where they would be enjoyed by everyone. He urged the Islanders to procure seeds from other tropical countries, and praised the effort of foreign naval officers who had brought in a variety of seeds on their last visit to Honolulu.

At the Royal Hawaiian Agricultural Society's next meeting, Hillebrand pushed even harder for the increased planting of trees and flowers in the Islands, and succeeded in raising the public's interest in their cultivation. He suggested to the citizens that the principal streets of Honolulu be lined with fine shade trees so that the high winds crossing the Pali would be checked. He stated, "King Street is broad and hot enough to be benefited for appearance and comfort's sake. There is another consideration which should urge us to a quick beginning—succulent branches of a living tree form an effective barrier to the spread of fire."

He then explained that the propagation of trees was a speedily rewarding task in Hawai'i's climate, citing examples of his own garden.

His acacia had grown from seed to 24 feet in little more than a year, melias had risen to 16 feet, and casuarinas to 10 feet. He indicated that, on his recommendation, the government had granted a water supply from its reservoir to citizens of Honolulu in order to stimulate home-owners to grow flowers and trees. His mother-in-law's caution that watering trees and plants was costly had not been forgotten.

Hillebrand also renewed his plea for importations of seeds from abroad. He gave as an example the fact that only two kinds of bananas grew in the Islands at the time, both poor varieties. Two more types had been recently brought in from Tahiti and they looked promising. He warned, however, that Islanders could not expect to receive imports without returning equivalents for what they received. Hillebrand sur-prised fellow members by announcing that he was already engaged in correspondence with botanical gardens in Paris, Rio de Janeiro, and Kew Gardens in London. Individual exchanges were praiseworthy, Hillebrand agreed, but what Hawai'i needed was an organized system supervised by an institution such as a botanical garden, which would collect in a limited space the production of the Hawaiian Islands and other countries. He explained:

> Our island florae, is not as rich as that of most other tropical countries, yet possesses the great charm of novelty. Only a few scattered species of Hawaiian plants are found in the richest botanical gardens of Europe and America. In all of them there exists a great desire to make acquisitions from this quarter, and they would undoubtedly make compensation in the most liberal manner. If this garden at the same time were managed as a nursery, where useful new importations could be first deposited, tried and studied, and from which they would be distributed gratis and with proper instructions to the population, it would become a source of great benefit. Besides, such an institution would raise our credit abroad, and throw a luster upon the government under which it originates.

This speech, designed to spark the interest of the royals and the city officials, did its trick. Soon after, Queen Emma leased thirty acres of land in Waikahalulu to William Hillebrand, which he immediately began to cultivate as a botanical garden.

He had not exaggerated when he spoke to the city officials about his established contacts to the world's most famous botanical gardens. His correspondence and exchange program with Sir William J. Hooker, director of Kew Gardens in London, proves that Sir William took a deep interest in Hillebrand's botanical endeavors and was his mentor. After Sir William's death in 1865, his son Joseph, the next director of Kew Gardens, continued the strong contact with his father's friend until Hillebrand's death.

Sir William knew he could rely on the young German doctor, who never tired of climbing the highest island mountains or sending out his delegates to discover new species. After an excursion to East Maui's old volcano Haleakalā (house of the sun), Hillebrand sent an excited note to Sir William, telling him,

> our mountain raspberry, which bears a fruit which, for
> size and juiciness I have not seen paralleled. A little
> more sweetness added to its succulency would make it a
> first rate fruit, and I trust, that this result may be attained
> by cultivation in the hands of experienced gardeners.

He promised seeds with a future shipment. Before he signed off with "my greatest respects, your most obedient servant W. H.," he asked Sir William, "Has my package of seeds, delivered by Dr. Newcomb, come to your hands yet?"

His father-in-law was the designated bearer of botanical goods that time around, but it appears that no ship and no traveler left Honolulu Harbor without being approached by Hillebrand to take along parcels of seeds, one or two Wardian cases with living plants, or a collection of dried species. Not even Dowager Queen Emma, on her diplomatic tour to England and Europe in 1865, was spared. Hillebrand proudly wrote to Sir William that the British ship of war, *Clio*, arrived "to scurry our beloved Queen to her first stopover, Panama." He reported that the queen graciously gave him permission to send along a collection of Hawaiian plants.

> Commissioner Mr. P. Synge, will take the
> Southampton steamer for England direct. Mr. Synge

has kindly promised me to take charge of the box...of
fern roots packed in powdered charcoal. The Queen
will return by the way of Panama and in all probability
Bishop Staley will have joined her in England, to
return with her. That would be a capital opportunity
to get living plants here in good condition. The Bishop
will do me the favor to call on you and take charge of
anything you may have for me. Aroids and orchids
would have a good chance to travel safely, not to forget
the ornamental Musaceae. Can you send seeds of the
Victoria Regina or even young plants? They could be
taken care of during the whole voyage.

When the *Clio* left Honolulu Harbor, Hillebrand's family and
friends jokingly said that William had stuffed every nook, niche, and
cannon barrel with seeds and plants. Not only were those personal
deliveries safer, they also saved the Agricultural Society money. To spare
Sir William a few pennies, thrifty Hillebrand advised him to send parcels
by West Indies steamers. He wrote, "The company carries articles free of
expenses across the Panama Isthmus."

Captain Ludwig Geerken, the German skipper of the barque *R. W.
Woods,* became Hillebrand's close friend and courier. The *Woods,* a regular
trader between Bremen and Honolulu, made one voyage either way each
year. As Hillebrand pointed out in a letter to Kew, "She never had a
longer passage from Bremen to Honolulu than 124 days." For the next
seventeen years, Captain Geerken regularly delivered Hillebrand's green
treasures to Kew Gardens.

six Botany and Medicine

IN JULY OF 1856, AT the sixth annual meeting of the Royal Hawaiian Agricultural Society, Hillebrand gave the address. In a speech so effective and visionary that the U.S. Department of Agriculture reprinted it in 1920, he spoke of the benefits of agriculture to mankind, particularly the benefits of forests. He cited the need for trees to affect the amount of rain and induce a cooler and wetter climate, and came down hard on cattle raisers who allowed their animals to roam free, thus destroying the existing forests. For Hillebrand, who came from a country where the prescribed punishment for tree mutilation in ancient times had been death, forestry was an important subject.

At this meeting he gave his first report on "Labor and Population." He spoke as a medical doctor and as a humanitarian, noting the decline of the native population because of infectious diseases. He strongly advocated

that the landless natives be given lots promptly so they could establish ʻāina
hoʻokūʻonoʻono (homesteads) and build stronger family ties.

Hillebrand had his rewards. His botanical genius was recognized by
his Royal Hawaiian Agricultural Society friends, as was his medical
knowledge and expertise by his colleagues. Thanks to his worldwide plant
exchange program, the first royal poinciana trees, glowing in scarlet or
orange colors, lined Honolulu's streets together with golden shower and
African tulip trees.

In a letter to the king in 1855, Hillebrand urged Kamehameha IV
to establish a hospital for sick and destitute native Hawaiians. Small private
hospitals were available for foreign residents, but none for the Hawaiian
population. Despite the king's active part in the work of organization and
Queen Emma's goodwill, three years passed before a temporary hospital
and dispensary opened on August 1, 1859, in a building on Honolulu's Fort
Street. In an almost unanimous vote, 17–2, the Board of Trustees elected
Dr. William Hillebrand as chief physician at a salary of $1,500 a year. He
held this position until his departure from Hawaiʻi eleven years later.

The new Queen's Hospital, build on eight acres of land at the corner
of Beretania and Punchbowl streets, was completed and occupied by the
end of 1860. Queen Emma's patronage, as well as subscriptions obtained
by the king, helped cover the cost of the building. After three years at
the helm of the hospital, Hillebrand stated that more than 6,000 patients
had applied for treatment and more than 16,000 prescriptions had been
furnished. Six hundred and twelve patients, 92 of them foreigners, had
been received at the hospital. Commenting on the attitude of the Native
Hawaiians, Hillebrand said it took a considerable amount of time before
the people realized that the hospital was a dispenser of unreserved charity.
They had feared that, after receiving its benefits, they would be forced to
pay in one way or another.

Nursing care for the sick was problematic at the beginning.
Without financial allowances for nurses or nurses' aids, Hillebrand chose
to accept the old Hawaiian custom of hiring kōkua (helpers). When a
Hawaiian patient entered Queen's Hospital, he was placed in a clean bed.
His sick bed-neighbor might have been old or young, even a baby. Now
the patient's kōkua—a mother, an aunt, or several close family members—
took over. They supplied the bedding, garments, and whatever else made
the patient feel comfortable. Kōkua usually came prepared with their own
mat and bedding as well, which they spread out next to the patient's bed.

A special room was provided for all *kōkua*. Here they could store their food supplies and cook the meals for the patients and themselves. When the laundry piled up, they pitched in and helped with the washing. The hospital park was a fine place to bleach the sheets. Other *kōkua* did the daily cleaning of the ward. This was far from Hillebrand's experience at the Berlin Charité Clinic, where already in 1840 the first trained nurses had been at work. But he soon found out that *kōkua* played an important part in a patient's recovery. For the next twenty-six years, *kōkua* did the nursing at Queen's Hospital. The first trained nurse, Mrs. Mary Adams, part-Hawaiian, was hired in 1888.

With the vision of a true botanist, Hillebrand looked at the twelve acres of the hospital garden, and after receiving free reign by Queen Emma, he had many fine, shade-giving trees planted. Two bombax trees (*Bombax ellipticum*), natives of Mexico, still grace the hospital grounds in the 21st century. Their hot pink and white blossoms are as beautiful as in Hillebrand's days.

Since 1859 Hillebrand had been a court-appointed private physician
of the royal family. By now he had become a *kamaʻāina* at heart. Letters to
his botanist friends around the world give proof of this. His admiration
for Queen Emma was great. He was at her side at the death of her first-
born child and helped her over her period of grief. When her husband,
Alexander Liholiho (Kamehameha IV), shot and wounded his private
secretary Henry Neilson in a mistaken jealous rage, Hillebrand was
called to take care of the victim, as well as the despondent Liholiho.
Despite the doctor's constant care, Neilson died of his wounds two and a
half years later.

The Hawaiian Medical Society, where Hillebrand served as vice-
president, praised his administrative abilities, which he conducted in his
quiet, unobtrusive ways. Because of his good standing with the royals and
his medical colleagues, he was able to initiate many new programs. One
of them was a compulsory quarantine of all incoming ships until they
could be checked for carriers of serious communicable diseases. Grave
concern was justified: Hillebrand had come upon the first cases of leprosy
on the island. In a report to the Board of Health, of which he was
commissioner, he stated that it was the Oriental leprosy which spread
alarmingly fast among the citizens of all islands:

> It will be the duty of the next Legislature to devise
> and carry out some efficient, and at the same time,
> humane measure, by which the isolation of those
> affected with the disease can be accomplished.

This act was approved by the king on January 3, 1865. How the
disease came to Hawaiʻi is unknown. Hawaiians called it *maʻi Pākē*,
Chinese sickness, because it was prevalent in China. Despite the looming
threat of the cruel disease, Hawaiian life went on as usual. Sunshine opti-
mism didn't give way to panic.

The Honolulu Advertiser reported about one of Hillebrand's inno-
vating medical surgeries: a new nose for a Chinese patient. By cutting
loose a piece of skin of the right size from the man's forehead and
pulling it down, the doctor formed a new nose. He then stretched the
skin of the forehead and sewed it together. The missing piece was hardly
noticeable. According to the *Advertiser*, this early plastic surgery was a
full success.

But not all Hillebrand news in the *Advertiser* was of a medical nature. Mrs. Hillebrand and Master William Francis let the people of Honolulu know that the doctor had a couple of jujube trees loaded with fruit growing in his garden. They wrote, "A delicious paste is made of the jujube fruit that delights the juveniles."

One month later, the Hillebrand family reported to the *Advertiser* that another colony of honeybees had swarmed in their garden and was successfully hived. There were now nine hives in their possession. The notice ended with a typical Hillebrand admonishment in a bit of German phrasing: "We should like to see more beekeeping increase."

Only a man with a strict daily schedule, and Hillebrand was known for that, would have had time left for beekeeping. By now he was the master of the Royal Hawaiian Society's garden and nursery with its thirty acres of fine, arable soil in Nu'uanu Valley. He lived in a modest house that was built for him on the grounds. From there he wrote to Sir W. J. Hooker at Kew in London:

> The garden…is already issuing a handsome appearance, although the first soil was turned over only a year ago… I hope it will do as much for the furtherance of botanical science as it certainly must do for the fruitful expansions of the resources of this country.

He rose early every morning to inspect the latest arrivals from other botanical gardens housed in the nursery. Had the seeds begun to sprout or were the insects, a neverending problem, at work again? This had happened the year before, when the nasty sugarcane borer did great damage. All sugarcane plants, which he had cultivated to test for the cane growers of Hawai'i, had to be removed immediately. But the damage was already done. Many of the surrounding plants had died.

After giving instructions to his well-trained gardeners, William would breakfast with Anna and their 7-year-old son William Francis in an arbor next to the house. The family loved these precious early hours of togetherness. Here Willie and his mother received their German lessons, preparing them for that one big trip to the doctor's home country.

Hillebrand drove himself to work in a one-horse gig, which he used to make his daily rounds to the Insane Asylum, Queen's Hospital, and his own office on the *mauka* (mountain side) corner of Fort and

Hotel Street. Late at night, when everybody was asleep, he wrote long, detailed letters to his mentor Sir William Hooker in London, or to his various botanist friends from Ceylon to Hannover in Germany. These were the men who shared his love for nature. They understood his despair when a long-awaited shipment of orchids from Java arrived insect-eaten and shriveled up, but they also shared his joy when the first plumeria and poinciana trees blossomed in the streets of Honolulu.

seven A Dream Come True

IN THE YEAR 1865, HILLEBRAND entered the ranks of privileged botanists. He joined those fortunate ones that were sent by sponsors on missions to faraway countries, well provided for with a generous budget.

Until now, in true scientific mode, Hillebrand had avoided any personal news in his correspondence with fellow botanists. But in April of 1865, he broke this rule. In a letter to Sir William Hooker at Kew Gardens, he wrote page upon page about the latest shipment of bromeliads, meyerias, and monstera deliciosa from Kew, England, which had arrived looking quite dead after 150 days at sea. He continued to report that to everyone's great surprise, those seemingly dead plants were now sending out tiny, green shoots. Finally, he didn't hold back any longer and sprang exciting news on Sir William: "I shall start in a month on a long voyage which will absent me from here for a year or more."

He explained:

> Of my impending voyage to China and the East Indies I entertain the most sanguine hopes. Our government, [illegible] being forced by the necessity of increasing the population and labor force of our Islands, has appointed me a Commissioner for immigration from these countries. I have carte blanche to visit China, Singapore, Java, Ceylon, Madras, Calcutta, Mauritius and the Philippine Islands, and on my return I shall probably see Japan also.
>
> My first duty is to send as many good agricultural laborers with their families from China, Madras, or Calcutta as can be procured. They will have to engage themselves for a time of five years—to be bound to a plantation or farm at the rate of wages ruling in this country. As labor is very light here and good laws give efficient protection to the laborer, there is little doubt but that most of the immigrants will be a permanent acquisition.
>
> My second duty will be to investigate and report on the measures resorted to in those countries against the Oriental leprosy, which disease, although of not more than 12 years standing here, is causing great alarm to this people.
>
> My third duty is to introduce useful plants and animals from those countries and for this purpose both our Agricultural Society and Government have placed funds at my disposal with considerable liberty. In furthering this objective which [illegible] lies nearest to my heart, you could lend me very effective assistance, if, in writing to your botanical and other friends in those countries, you would just mention my name in a few short lines. Dr. Thwaites and the *Cinchona* trees in the Peredeniya Gardens are most prominent in my view. Now I expect to get the spice trees, the mangosteen, the teak, [illegible] from their native countries. It is a realization of a dream which I have long carried with me.

You may be sure that I shall pick up every fern that
comes in my way…

Hillebrand knew this was a plum assignment which thousands of
botanists could only dream of: a ship at his disposal, the routes up to his
own digression, an annual salary of $6,000, as well as a $500 budget for
botanical purposes. He also had permission to take along his wife Anna
and their 12-year-old son, William Francis. The Islands' native population
had dwindled to below 70,000. Plantation owners demanded that
immigrant laborers be brought in. But they also remembered their
failed attempt in 1852 to bring Chinese laborers to the Islands. Most of
those men, not being used to agricultural work, had left the plantations
before their contract expired. Hillebrand promised to procure healthy,
hardworking farmhands.

He again committed himself to a long voyage despite his precarious
health. During the last years, he lived his life according to the latest
European medical research on treatment of pulmonary tuberculosis, and
spent as much time as possible in fresh air and sunshine. When working in
his garden, or going surf fishing with William Francis at Waikīkī, he would
take off his shirt to let the sun "heal" his lungs. This caused his English
friends to say that Hillebrand "went Hawaiian," while his family jokingly
called him *kanaka* (Hawaiian man) because of his deep, brown tan. Despite
the special care he took, he often suffered from chest-colds and fever.

• • •

In late April of 1865, the 15-year-old clipper ship *Sea Serpent*, under
the command of Captain Winsor and a 17-man crew, left Honolulu
Harbor for Hong Kong. The Hillebrand family and their Hawaiian-
Chinese interpreter, Ah Fat, waved *aloha* to their friends that had gathered
at the pier. The *Serpent*'s foredeck was loaded with plant-filled Wardian cases,
which William Hillebrand intended for trade at Asian botanical gardens.

But botany, no matter how close to Hillebrand's heart, had to take a
back seat once the *Serpent* arrived in Hong Kong. Hillebrand immediately
embarked on his first duty—laborer procurement. He soon realized that
his intent to go out into China's villages to hire workers was impossible.
The vastness of the country and the difficulty and danger of traveling
to remote areas had been underestimated. In addition, because of his

interpreter's diffidence and helplessness, Ah Fat became more of a hindrance than help. Hillebrand had to look for assistance elsewhere. In a long letter to the Hawaiian Minister of Interior, he wrote about the difficulty of the assignment, but also of his good fortune to have been introduced to a former German missionary. William Lobscheid, a learned sinologue, had agreed to assist him in his endeavors.

Hillebrand wrote,

> His (Lobscheid) object in lending himself to these transactions is by no means one of pecuniary gain. Having witnessed the many atrocious cruelties connected with the coolie trade, as conducted by private speculators he seriously set himself about finding a remedy.
>
> But, as he told me, "he soon came to the conclusion that it was useless to try to swim against the current of the world."
>
> If other countries needed laborers, they would contrive to get them, no matter by what means. The only feasible remedy seemed to him to take hold of the matter himself and direct it in its proper, legitimate channel.

With the help of Reverend Lobscheid, Hillebrand signed up 528 Chinese workers, including 96 women and 10 children, and placed them on two vessels. As explanation for his actions, he cited an incident that happened a month earlier, when a vessel with 600 Chinese on board arrived on the coast of Sumatra with 27 dead and 66 cases of illness. Poor ventilation and a lack of lighting may have been some of the causes for the tragedy, as he had learned from the Hong Kong harbormaster.

He was full of praise at the industriousness he encountered in China. "It seems to be one vast beehive in which there are no drones. One cannot help coming to the conclusion that such a population would be a mighty help in developing the hidden resources of any country."

Feeling like a true *kama'āina*, he wrote proudly to the Minister of Interior that in China, "our" Islands are looked upon more favorably than any other country in matters of immigration. He explained that Hawai'i was well-known under the Chinese name of Tan-heang-shan, a word that meant Sandalwood (fragrant wood) Islands. Its closeness to China and Kin Shan (California), as well as the fact that some well-off Chinese already lived there, helped to recruit laborers. Hillebrand cited the many countries that had procured Chinese men to build railroads or to work on the Suez Canal. He was convinced he hired the right people for Hawai'i.

While port regulations prescribed that emigrant ships for Honolulu had to be provisioned for fifty-one days during the southwest monsoon and seventy-five days during the northeast monsoon, he directed Mr. Booth of Bourjean, Hubner & Co. to place an additional 75 piculs (Asian weight, equivalent to 133 lbs.) of rice on board and to increase the water rations. On July 20, 1865, the Chilean barque *Alberto*, left Hong Kong before nightfall with the first transport of approximately 250 Chinese

In 1865 Hillebrand was successful in his efforts to import contract labor from China to support the expanding sugar industry.

COURTESY OF BISHOP MUSEUM ARCHIVES

laborers for Honolulu. Two weeks later, a second vessel, the British ship *Roscoe*, followed with about 270 Chinese on board. Thanks to his organizational talent and tenaciousness, Hillebrand had achieved an enormous task in a relatively short time. These 530 Chinese became an important part of the Hawaiian culture.

Before closing his letter to the Board of Immigration, Hillebrand had to put in a word for himself. He informed the Council that the agreed amount of $6,000 salary for him would not suffice. He foresaw an absence from Hawai'i of at least eighteen months with extensive travel in China, and therefore requested a salary increase to the sum of $7,500. He reminded the Minister of Interior that, after all, he would not return empty-handed: "What good will result to our country by those new importations of animals and plants, is quite beyond calculation yet."

As Hillebrand continued his travel, it can be assumed that Kamehameha IV granted his request.

eight Return to Hawai'i

WHEN THE SECOND SHIP, THE *Roscoe*, filled with Chinese laborers for Hawai'i, left Hong Kong Harbor in August of 1865, Hillebrand must have sighed with relief. His most important task had been accomplished and his Prussian sense of duty was appeased. Trustworthy, reliable Mr. Lobscheid, Hillebrand's contact in Hong Kong, had promised to take care of future laborer procurement for the Islands if the need should arise. Hillebrand was certain that the Hawaiian government would be satisfied with his swift conduct of their affairs.

He was now free to pursue the other two objectives on his agenda—searching for the latest treatment of leprosy and acquiring plants and animals for the Islands. For the latter he had one tree in mind, the red cinchona. The tree was named in honor of Condesa de Chincon, who legend says was cured of a fever in 1638 by a preparation of the tree's bark. At her instigation, the bark was collected for malaria sufferers and later exported to Spain. Indians had long used it for medicinal purposes.

In 1842, when the effectiveness of quinine as prevention against malaria was officially established, the lure of the red cinchona tree and its magical potency became known worldwide. By 1860 the hunt for seeds or young plants of the "wonder tree" was on. Plant hunters from all continents set out for the Andes, where the trees grew at high elevations. Hillebrand, too far away from the Andes, had another source in mind. He had heard of a British plantation in Ceylon that had successfully raised the trees. He hoped a kind word from Sir William J. Hooker to Dr. George Thwaites, the plantation director, would help him to obtain a few young plants. Always on the lookout for possible sources of income for Hawai'i, Hillebrand might have dreamed of a future pharmaceutical venture for the Islands.

Before leaving China he visited a leprosarium, a retreat not far from Hong Kong. But he did not see any sovereign remedy that would be superior to the Hawaiian treatments. He also didn't share the popular belief in southern China that leprosy spread from the decomposing urine of the lepers. He set his hopes on Ceylon and India, where large leprosy retreats had been established.

Perhaps not by accident, Hillebrand's future ports of call were well-known for their botanical gardens. Pondicherry, 126 kilometers south of Madras, offered not only local flora, but also a medicinal herb garden of importance. Calcutta's botanical garden, founded in 1787, boasted a large collection of indigenous and non-indigenous plants. Hillebrand was especially interested in its tree collection with its enormous 200-year-old banyan tree. Considered the world's largest with a circumference of 330 meters, he was fascinated by the tree's 600 long, sinewy roots reaching for the ground. Hillebrand was in botanist heaven, a view that his wife didn't share. Properly dressed Victorian-style in black silk and a corseted waist, she was overcome by India's heat and humidity during their third visit to Calcutta's garden. Unwell and homesick for O'ahu, she vowed that this would be the last garden to which her husband would take her.

Whatever botanical establishment Hillebrand visited, he was welcomed by the directors. For many years he had been in correspondence with Dr. Thomas Anderson, director of Calcutta's botanical garden. The two men formed a friendship that lasted a lifetime.

Laborer procurement in India did not pan out as Hillebrand had hoped. He missed the well-organized approach of Mr. Lobscheid in Hong Kong, and did not like the selection methods of the traders in Calcutta. The Indian approach towards leprosy didn't offer anything new either. He set his hopes on Ceylon and on the island of Mauritius, where he planned to see the Jardin des Pamplemousses (Garden of Grapefruits), the world's first tropical botanical garden established in 1745.

But like years ago in the Philippines, India's sultry climate didn't agree with the doctor's health. A persistent cough and fever at the end of his stay in Calcutta made him realize that he had to give up his travel plans to Ceylon and Mauritius. It was time to head back to their home in the Sandwich Islands. Reluctantly he planned his return trip to O'ahu.

Once more his wife had to endure heat, humidity, and tropical inconveniences. William had arranged a stopover at Java. Buitenzorg, the Dutch botanical garden, which he had visited for the first time in 1848 on his way from Australia to Manila, was too important to be bypassed. Here he had seen the flowering trees which so impressed him that he had many different kinds imported for the beautification of Honolulu.

Buitenzorg ("free from care"), a magnificent garden at the foot of two volcanoes, was laid out in 1817 by Sir Stamford Raffles. It was so enchanting that Anna Hillebrand forgot about her vow never to visit another botanical garden again. She spent days observing the luscious, exotic plants. At an excursion into a tea plantation surrounding Buitenzorg, Anna did what she should have done months before—she took off the tight, long-sleeved, corseted waist part of her dress, and continued the visit in her camisole. "It was the only way to go," as she wrote to her mother.

Hillebrand's shopping list for Java was large—camphor, cinnamon, jackfruit and litchi, eugenias and banyans. He filled eight Wardian cases and ordered more to be shipped later. Shoots of the red cinchona, given to him at Buitenzorg, delighted him no end. A pair of Java deer joined the Chinese deer and quails already aboard the ship. Not all the new acquisitions were wise by today's standard, but 150 years ago, botanists considered themselves nature's missionaries and Hillebrand couldn't be more fervent.

Young William Francis, Hillebrand's son, described the family's return voyage to the Sandwich Islands as "somewhat rough and gloomy," during which his mother was seasick most of the time. He had vivid recollections of his assignment to help feed and care for the birds and deer on that seven-week trip from Hong Kong to Honolulu via San Francisco.

William "Willie" Francis, Hillebrand's eldest son.

The *Hawaiian Gazette* for July 1866 reported that Dr. William Hillebrand had forwarded ten Wardian cases from Singapore, nine from Calcutta, one from Ceylon, eight from Java, and two from China. They wrote about the importations of camphor, cinnamon, mandarin orange, Chinese plum, Java plums, and the considerable number of other useful or ornamental plants.

Willie's charges—the imported carrion crows; gold finches; Japanese finches; linnets; mynah birds; Chinese quail; ricebirds; Indian sparrows; golden, silver, and Mongolian pheasants; and the deer from China and Java—were now the talk of Honolulu.

nine Home Again in Hawai'i

HONOLULU NEVER LOOKED BETTER TO the Hillebrands as when they returned after nearly two years of travel in Asia. They were home again in the kingdom they had come to love. William hoped to regain his health in Hawai'i's mild climate as he had done seventeen years ago. Their house and garden at North Vineyard had been looked after by William's brother Hermann, who had joined William four years earlier. Hermann had become a prosperous dairy farmer on O'ahu, and was the husband of Elisabeth Bishop, missionary Sereno Bishop's daughter.

The family returned to a changed Hawaiian administration. During their absence, R. C. Wyllie, minister of foreign affairs, had passed away. Hillebrand mourned the death of the man who had met him with much friendliness when he arrived in 1850. Wyllie's successor, Charles de Varigny, was a former minister of finance and well-known to Hillebrand.

While they always conducted their conversation in an amiable French, politically they did not share the same opinions.

An enormous task lay before William Hillebrand. The government wanted extensive reports on the business he had conducted during his travel. The medical community eagerly awaited a speech on leprosy treatments in Asia. Thirty-four Wardian cases of plants, as well as several thousand seed packages, needed to be taken care of immediately.

Again it was Hillebrand's ability to delegate and organize that helped him to overcome the obstacle. With the help of his well-trained botanical volunteer force, he took care of the plant acquisitions and the many animals he had brought back. Hermann Holstein, German manager of the Royal Hawaiian Agricultural Society's botanical garden on Maui, a trusted friend and excellent gardener, had been in charge of all botanical matters during Hillebrand's absence. He received the precious cinchona shoots for propagation in the Maui garden. Others, like Honolulu volunteer Benoni Davidson, took new plants home and nursed them to a healthy growth. Some of these trees and shrubs later on adorned the hospital grounds, as Mrs. Mary Davidson told *The Honolulu Advertiser* in 1923.

Indian mynah birds and ricebirds quickly felt at home on the Islands. Did they take care of gnats and mosquitoes? Perhaps not to the extent Hillebrand had hoped. The *Hawaiian Annual* reported in 1901 that mynahs had become a big nuisance. They not only devoured the eggs of native birds, but also robbed the fruit growers of their harvest. Figs were the mynahs' favorite fruit. Whatever happened to the two imported pairs of China and Java deer remains a mystery. They could have easily fallen prey to hunters.

Hillebrand had hardly returned to his work at the hospital and the Insane Asylum, when he was called to the King's Palace. Kamehameha V, who was now over 300 lbs., was in urgent need of Hillebrand's medical attention. The German doctor's quiet reassurance and his interesting reports of travel episodes helped Prince Lot to get well faster.

While Hillebrand tried to resolve his workload, his wife Anna prepared their homestead for a new family member. Her seasickness turned out to be pregnancy.

The recurrence of his tuberculosis had made William Hillebrand aware of his fragile health. How many more years would he have left to work on his book, *Flora of the Hawaiian Islands*? He had worked on this project since his arrival on the Sandwich Islands and had decided long ago that this book would be his legacy to Hawai'i. As soon as his health improved, he continued with renewed vigor to collect indigenous phanerogams and vascular cryptogams. If some of O'ahu's hills were too steep for him to climb, he sent his son Willie and his young friends on the excursion. They didn't always return from their plant hunt with the desired success. Despite Hillebrand's written instructions, they would forget to mark down the precise location of their find, or bring back shriveled plants that hadn't been properly preserved. The ensuing reprimands from his father may have been a reason why young Willie decided not to become a botanist by profession.

Because of his Asia trip, Hillebrand missed out on meeting a famous visitor to Hawai'i. Mark Twain, who arrived on the Islands on March 18, 1866, unknowingly gave credit to several of Hillebrand's achievements. In one of his first letters to San Francisco, Twain wrote about Honolulu's beautiful shade trees with their dense foliage that sun could scarcely penetrate. He raved about "luxurious banks and thickets of flowers" in front of houses and "huge-bodied, wide-spreading forest trees, with strange names and stranger appearance—trees that cast a shadow like a thundercloud, and were able to stand alone without being tied to green poles."

The doctor's heart would have leapt for joy had he been able to read Twain's statements about the city, which Hillebrand had experienced as a more barren place sixteen years earlier. Twain's report on Honolulu's water system would have been another reward for the doctor.

Twain wrote,

> The water is pure, sweet, cool, clear as crystal, and
> comes from a spring in the mountains, and is distributed
> all over the town through leaden pipes. You can find a
> hydrant spurting away at the bases of three or four trees
> in a single yard sometimes, so plenty and cheap is this
> excellent water. Only twenty four dollars a year supplies
> a whole household with limitless quantity of it.

That certainly was a monument to William's tenacity. Twain wrote more about water when he described the slender-necked, large-bodied, gourd-shaped earthenware vessels, which kept drinking water cool. Every Honolulu household owned one or two of these receptacles. As they were manufactured in Germany, and used to be prevalent in Hillebrand's native Westphalia, they were most certainly another of his innovations for Hawai'i.

ten The Great Quake

ON THE 27TH OF MARCH 1868 at 4 P.M., a series of strong earthquakes shook the Big Island of Hawai'i. Kīlauea, known as the "restless" volcano, had been unusually full of lava for weeks. Now it looked threatening.

The island's inhabitants, used to a fair amount of mini tremors, grew concerned when the shocks became more frequent and severe. By nightfall the people of Hilo were frightened enough to rush outdoors, spending a fearful night away from their houses. They counted over 1,000 shocks before morning broke.

What followed then was described by an excited Hillebrand in a letter to Sir Joseph D. Hooker at Kew Gardens:

> On April 2nd, while the fire in Kilauea seemed
> to recede, a most terrific shock occurred, which was

felt here in Honolulu and laid prostrate, or threw off
the foundation, all walls and most houses in Kau
(Big Island).

The quake's estimated magnitude of 7.9 was large even by San Andreas
standards. He went on:

> All the fissures described in my report were produced
> then, amongst which, that most extraordinary one,
> which split the side of the mountain and went down
> to the level plain with enormous masses of dirt and
> water—the mudflow of Kapapala. The great stellated
> fissure in Kahuku through which five days later the
> lava broke, must have been first opened by this shock.
> Immediately after it, the sea receded and soon returned
> in an enormous wave 40-50 ft. high which ran over
> the tops of the coconut palms and swept away every
> village on the southern coast, destroying about 60 lives
> and disabling many poor fellows.

Hillebrand reported about the 15-20 times that the sea receded and
returned again, before resuming its "equilibrium." He wrote,

> These waves reached California and Oregon 5 hrs
> later. But strange to say, here in Honolulu it was hardly
> noticed, and was even quite insignificant in the north-
> ern part of the Big Island. During the four days follow-
> ing the great shock more than 2000 after shocks were
> counted in Kau. In Kapapala the ground was in incessant
> motion, swaggering to and fro like the sea, so that people
> became seasick.
>
> On the night between the 3rd and 4th, three
> shocks occurred which were even felt in Honolulu.
> On the 7th the lava burst out of the great star shaped
> fissures in Kahuku and reached the sea in three hours.

A natural phenomenon of such dimension attracted William
Hillebrand as physician and naturalist. He couldn't wait to offer his medical

assistance to the people of the Big Island and to study this natural disaster. But he wasn't the only one who wanted to rush to Hawai'i. Hundreds of Hawaiians were anxious to find out if their relatives had survived the catastrophe. Kamehameha V, his foreign minister Charles de Varigny, and Bishop Louis Maigret made a first attempt to reach their constituents two days after the disaster. But storms had cut off the island and the group was stranded for four days on Maui.

Hillebrand, after a ten-day wait, finally got on board the crowded interisland steamer *Kīlauea*. Amazed but undeterred by the devastation he encountered at his arrival, he immediately helped take care of injured Hawaiians at a makeshift first aid station. Many people had suffered head injuries and broken bones from falling masonry and wooden beams.

Only when his medical services weren't needed anymore did Hillebrand give in to his scientific curiosity, conducting lava tests at Kapāpala. Tremors still shook the ground, and many times he and his group of friends had to hold on to a bush or tree so that they wouldn't lose their balance. During the next twenty-four hours they counted nineteen strong aftershocks.

Their first night was spent close to Kīlauea's crater, which was entirely devoid of lava, no incandescence anywhere. During their second night, detonations were heard again and white vapors of steam issued from the ground in a hundred places. Hillebrand wrote, "In many places the heat was so great that it would forbid the touch of the bare hand."

Close to the crater, the group encountered the grotesque shapes of a dense forest that had been overrun and destroyed by lava. It was an eerie, but interesting phenomenon for the botanist and he studied it carefully.

> Wherever the lava had met a tree of some size, it had surrounded it with a perfect mould which either still held the smoldering remains of the trunk, or exhibited hollow cylinders bearing on the inside the markings of the bark or of the tree. The leaf stalk scars of fern-trees were almost perfect.

A continuous line of white and yellow smoke forced the group to retreat in a hurry.

His tests of Kīlauea and Mauna Loa lava consistency showed it to be rich in olivae and as light and porous as that of Kīlauea's 1840 eruption. He came to the conclusion that the two volcanoes must have become interconnected. In his words: the two volcanoes had "established a communication." This theory existed for a long time, although it is now thought to be incorrect. Deeper stresses, at about 10 kilometers depth, are more likely the reason.

In his letter to Kew, Hillebrand added an interesting post scriptum,

> The extraordinary liquidity of the lava was
> another remarkable phenomena. It ran over a distance
> of 15 miles, down a slope of probably not more than 8
> degrees in less than 4 hrs. Capt. Brown, on whose
> ranch the eruption broke out and who, with his family,
> had to flee for dear life, says that the lava ran at the rate
> of 10 miles an hour. Brown's residence was buried
> under the lava.

Hillebrand's earthquake reports to Kew as well as his articles in the *Honolulu Gazette* made world press. Educational institutions and clubs from all over the United States requested his lectures. In October of 1868, he spoke to a full house at San Francisco's famous Olympic Club. Two weeks later on October 21, his audience would experience the great San Francisco earthquake of 1868.

eleven Island Excursions

JOHN M. LYDGATE, BORN IN 1854, was the son of a sugarcane plantation manager on the Sandwich Islands. Lydgate and William Francis (Willie) Hillebrand had become close friends at Honolulu's Punahou School, where they received an excellent education under the chief guidance of professor D. W. Alexander.

During his visits to the Hillebrand home and garden, John Lydgate showed an unusual interest in botany for a 14-year-old boy. Unlike Willie, Lydgate couldn't wait to go on botanical expeditions with his friend's father. Hillebrand was delighted to have a young, enthusiastic companion on his often strenuous and sometimes risky excursions. The strong teenager helped carry the field equipment and pitch the tent, and in exchange received a thorough botanical education.

John Lydgate, who later became a minister, reminisced often about their collecting excursions and the tremendous knowledge he gained during that time. He became a great admirer of the doctor and a true friend. Years later, after Hillebrand's return to Europe, Lydgate became the botanist's reliable collector and messenger on the Islands. Parcels with seeds and plants went back and forth between the two men. In one of his recollections, Lydgate described Hillebrand as

> always a gentleman in the largest sense of the word, genial, kindly, natural and easy, but never common or coarse in the slightest degree. He was most companionable and interesting, yet always in a dignified and courteous way. He was unvaryingly patient, as he sometimes had need to be, with a more or less irresponsible boy like me. He took kindly and fatherly interest in me, which outran the time being, and was very helpful to me.

He further praised Hillebrand:

> Intellectually and socially he was a man of most varied and valuable attainments, well versed along many lines, and at home at any subject, and in any surroundings. He was undoubtedly one of the most valuable men who have made the Islands their home, and his memory will be treasured as such.

Lydgate also gave an account about the memorable hours he spent in the lovely, but simple Hillebrand home. He described their large garden as a wonderful green oasis where in 1868, the family's newborn baby boy Henry Thomas cooed in his crib under the canopy of a large catalpa tree.

• • •

Botanizing on the other Hawaiian Islands was not without its challenges. Hillebrand remembered that his first trip to Kona, Hawai'i, in the early 1850s had taken nine uncomfortable days at sea. A newspaper report of one of those trips listed 270 passengers on board, plus 20 turkeys, 30 pigs, 75 chickens, 30 dogs, 1 pair of oxen, 1 mule, 14 cords wood, 11 canoes, etc. By 1860 interisland trips still lacked speed and comfort.

One of their plant hunts took Hillebrand and John Lydgate to the isle of Lāna'i. Over the years the Sandwich Islands had attracted many colorful people. The man the two botanists were going to meet on this trip was one of the most colorful of all. Walter Murray Gibson claimed to have been born to an English noble family in 1822, aboard a storm-tossed vessel in the Bay of Biscay. He was convinced that through an unlucky switch on the ship, he was handed over to a poor farmer's wife who had given birth to a boy the same night. Always trying to better his station in life, he had undertaken many business ventures, not always respectable. By 1880 he had advanced from ex-communicated Mormon missionary to minister of foreign affairs of Hawai'i.

When the two men met tall, gaunt Gibson, he was still master of his big, but primitive ranch on the isle of Lāna'i. Soon after he would return to Honolulu to become one of the most powerful and controversial men in Hawai'i's history. For five days Gibson played host to the botanists. He couldn't wait for his guests to return to the ranch from their daylong excursions. Gibson loved to talk, and enjoyed his visitors, who had no other choice but to listen to their host's tall stories, usually told in Hawaiian. Over a meal of roast mutton, boiled rice, molasses and coffee, he entertained them with wildly embroidered tales about his travel to the Dutch Indies.

On one of his Lāna'i hikes, Hillebrand discovered a "striking and rather showy plant"—a very rare lobelia. He named it *Cyanea gibsonii* in honor of his eccentric host. Walter Murray Gibson was delighted.

Another excursion brought Hillebrand and Lydgate to Moloka'i, the island that had become synonymous with leprosy. At Kalaupapa, on the northern coast of the island, the first group of lepers arrived from Honolulu in January 1866. Hillebrand had opted for a more humane settlement on O'ahu, but the majority of the Board of Health chose Moloka'i. The Board appointed Rudolph W. Meyer, a sugarcane planter and rancher, and long time resident of that isle, as agent and overseer of the settlement.

Contrary to their visit to Lāna'i, Hillebrand and Lydgate felt completely at ease at the Meyer ranch in Kala'e. Meyer, who was happily married to a Hawaiian chiefess, reared a large family. Lydgate described the rancher as "a well educated German immigrant." Conversations between the rancher and the doctor were conducted mostly in German. As a longtime friend of the doctor, Meyer belonged to Hillebrand's botanical volunteer force. Like so many others in Hawai'i, he was trained by Hillebrand to look out for any unusual plants or trees.

From the Meyer ranch, Hillebrand and Lydgate climbed the summit of the Pelekunu mountain ridge and the *pali* (cliffs) along Kala'e. For a person with tubercular damage to his lungs, this was not an easy undertaking. But for Hillebrand, the wanderer and explorer, it was just another challenge.

Evenings at the ranch were dedicated to music. Meyer's piano was a magnet for the doctor, as were all pianos. Despite his complaint that the ones in the Hawaiian Islands were out of tune due to humidity, he couldn't stay away from them. Playing German songs or his beloved opera arias for the assembled Meyer family gave the days a festive ending.

John Lydgate had another opportunity to admire the doctor's linguistic talents. At an excursion to Lahaina, Maui, they lived in one of Murray Gibson's beachside grass houses. Monsieur Oudinot, a French bachelor who cultivated grapes, was well-known in the Islands for his excellent wines. For Oudinot, a visit from Hillebrand was a much desired opportunity to get answers to his numerous botanical questions. For instance, had the doctor heard of any new insect-resistant grapevines developed anywhere in the world? And what was the best way to eradicate the insect pest?

Over a good meal and an excellent glass of wine at Oudinot's home, the two men had long discussions in French about the vintner's problems. Of course, the evenings also ended with Hillebrand playing the piano for his host.

• • •

After William Hillebrand's return to Europe, Lydgate continued to send him interesting plants which he found on his wanderings. This enabled the doctor to complete his collection of the *Flora of the Hawaiian Islands*. Hillebrand valued these contributions highly. As evidence of his interest and regard, he made up a type collection for the young man and sent it to him from Germany. Too young to really appreciate the enormous work that had gone into the preparation of this gift, Lydgate left the well-made box at his parents' home when he went off to college.

Fifteen years later, he found it undamaged in the attic of the house. He described how he opened the box and saw the reams and reams of dried plants, "every one of them bringing back thrilling memories of excursions to mountain peaks and valley glens; the high light touches of a lifetime; all carefully labeled with name and location, and laid away between files of old newspapers."

Lydgate realized that such a valuable collection should go to a place where it was properly appreciated, especially since there was no other such collection in the country. He handed it over to Mr. C. N. Forbes, botanical curator at the Bishop Museum. Within a few days, he received an enthusiastic letter from Mr. Forbes stating that the collection contained 566 specimens, almost all in perfect shape. Would John Lydgate agree to the sum of $500? Of course, he did. Lydgate called it a scientific treasure trove. He often visited the museum and remembered his extraordinary friend and mentor.

twelve Time for Decisions

SOCIAL LIFE FOR THE FOREIGN residents on the Sandwich Islands had changed considerably by 1860. Gone were the days when Honolulu women were in constant search of new variations to prepare beef, the only available meat then. Now that they had their choice of several grocery stores where they could buy chicken, potted meats, and even *pâté*, dinner invitations to friends went out more often.

A festive evening at the house of Hawai'i's foreign minister Charles de Varigny and his wife, Louise, would include a truly delicious French meal of galantines, turkey, fish, lobster salad, custard creams, and cakes to delight the guests. Madame de Varigny claimed to be Honolulu's gastronomic innovator who created a taste for filet mignon steak, a dish unknown before on the Sandwich Islands.

Anna and William Hillebrand's circle of friends had grown large. Princess Bernice Pauahi Bishop and Charles R. Bishop were frequent visitors to the Hillebrand home, as was John Mott-Smith, Hawai'i's first dentist, and his wife. This trusted business partner would become Hillebrand's financial administrator after his return to Europe.

The Hillebrands reciprocated their friends' invitations with hearty Westphalian meals. The doctor made sure their garden never ran out of carrots, green beans, cabbage, and onions so that Anna could prepare his favorite Westphalian bacon and vegetable stews. Social gatherings at the Hillebrand home quite often took place around a big, steaming casserole terrine filled with one of Anna's delicious concoctions. The aroma of fresh garden vegetables and herbs would fill the small house on Vineyard Drive. In the late 1860s, if Anna didn't find time to bake William's favorite Westphalian apple cake, Herr Horn, a German baker, catered cakes and ice cream to the parties. His dark, crusty pumpernickel (Westphalian dark rye bread) would always be served with Anna's stews.

The Hillebrands had many reasons to be content with their lives in the Sandwich Islands. Steamer voyages to San Francisco had shortened travel time to nine days, which made short sojourns to California possible. Anna's parents, Dr. and Mrs. Wesley Newcomb, had taken up residence in Oakland, across San Francisco Bay. William's brother, Henry, who had immigrated to Texas and married Clara Kleeberg (sister of Congressman Kleeberg), had also moved to Oakland. Family reunions, meetings with fellow botanist Dr. Henry N. Bolander in San Francisco, and a two-week botanizing trip into the Sierra filled their short vacations.

William Hillebrand's correspondence and plant exchange with fellow botanists worldwide had grown enormously. By now he was widely known as a palm tree expert. One of those who relied heavily on William's knowledge was His Royal Highness King Georg V of Hannover, cousin of Queen Victoria. His beautiful Baroque garden in Herrenhausen with its cascades, grottos, waterfalls, and fountains, also boasted a unique palm garden. For years the garden master, Hermann Wendland, had obtained plants from William or asked for his advice when it came to new palm acquisitions. For William it was an amusing fact that the king of Hannover, whose subject he had been during his student days in Goettingen, now asked him for advice. But it was an invitation from Cambridge, Massachusetts, to spend a year with professor Asa Gray, Harvard's eminent botanist that filled William with greatest pride.

Yet worries plagued him. He had always downplayed his own fragile health, but in 1868, it was Anna's health he was concerned about. After the birth of Harry, she didn't regain her usual strength. She had lost weight and felt tired. On their last return from California, Anna came down with a chest cold that didn't seem to go away. What if she, too, had become infected with tuberculosis? If so, how much longer would they be able to stay in Hawai'i before they had to search for a cure in the United States? William was worried.

As much as he had looked forward to seeing his beloved Westphalia again, a possible departure from Hawai'i now loomed heavily over him. Parting from the Islands where he had found fulfillment and happiness for many years would be hard. He loved his work at the hospital and had grown fond of many of his patients.

For a botanist to abandon his green treasures, which he had nursed from seed to maturity, would be equally as heartbreaking. The latest report from Hermann Holstein about the cinchona cultivation at the botanical garden on Maui was encouraging. The young plants had grown to 4 feet in height. Could he leave all this behind? Then there was the neverending excitement of finding still another undiscovered botanical species for his *Flora of the Hawaiian Islands.* This passion to pursue that one elusive species would be exceedingly difficult to give up.

Many more decisions needed to be made. William Francis, his eldest son, was going on sixteen. He had reached the age where a good college should be chosen. Hillebrand had set his mind on the University of Heidelberg in Germany. The quaint city at the Neckar River seemed to be the right environment for the young boy who had lived a sheltered life on the Sandwich Islands.

In the end he reminded himself of his life's motto: "nil desperandum" (never despair). He pushed his troubling thoughts aside and hoped that the announced visit of Dr. and Mrs. Newcomb to Honolulu would help Anna to recover and give the Hillebrands a chance to delay their departure.

thirteen Leaving Hawai'i

"BOTANIZING ON OUR ISLANDS IS not without considerable danger,"
Hillebrand explained in a letter to Sir Joseph D. Hooker in October of
1869. "Only imagine my being obliged to descend a steep talus of at least
70°, which had to be done chiefly by swinging from the roots of one tree
to the branches of the next one below, and that from a height of 2000 ft.
above the deep gorge below."

His dangerous excursion, which took place in the Ka'ala range
(Wai'anae) of O'ahu, had its rewards. He found a viola that surprised him
by its size and beautiful, snow-white waxy flowers. Unfortunately, it seemed
to grow only on the dangerous razor-backed ridges of the mountains.

His letter goes on:

> Three new species amongst which a terebinthaceous
> tree [a small tree whose cut bark yields a turpentine],

and several of our rarest plants, as the *Alsinidendron*
trinerve, have been the reward of much hard climbing.
I shall send you of all by the first party that shall leave
for Europe and be willing to carry the bundles.

He did not tell Joseph D. Hooker that the Hillebrands were going to
leave the Sandwich Islands. Not yet made public, they nevertheless began to
prepare for the move. William had watched Anna with concern during her
parents' visit to Honolulu. While her stepfather Dr. Wesley Newcomb
dredged Honolulu Harbor for seashells, Anna's mother Helen helped her
take care of little Harry. For a while, Anna's pale face regained some of its
former healthy complexion, but her tubercular symptoms remained.
Together with the Newcombs, the Hillebrands decided that Anna needed
to see a specialist on the U.S. mainland soon. William Francis had received a
letter of acceptance from Cornell University preparatory from where he
would go on to Heidelberg.

After twenty years, breaking up residency in Hawai'i was more
complicated than first thought. Kamehameha V's health was again in a
precarious state. William, who had been called to his side many times,
knew that the king had only a short time to live. Shouldn't he be with
the royal during his final hour? Then there was his joint drugstore venture
with Dr. John Mott-Smith. Hillebrand wasn't going to relinquish this still-
flourishing business. Papers needed to be drawn up to give full power to
Mott-Smith whom he trusted completely. He appointed him executor of
his financial affairs in Hawai'i and the U.S.

Considering these time-consuming preparations, William decided
to send Anna and his two sons ahead to the East Coast of the United
States. The decision had not been an easy one as they foresaw a twelve-
month separation until their reunion in Cambridge, Massachusetts. In
spring of 1870, Anna, William Francis, and Henry waved a tearful *aloha* to
William and their friends at the pier. Anna, who had only spent her
childhood years in the United States, had always been a loyal American.
But on that spring day in Honolulu, she painfully realized her heartfelt
connection to the Hawaiian Islands. For the rest of her life, she would
long for the tranquility of her home in Nu'uanu Valley and the Island
friends she left behind.

• • •

Over the years, work at Queen's Hospital and other medical engagements had demanded much of William's time. With the appointment of Dr. McKibben as his assistant and future successor, he was able to slowly disengage himself from his many responsibilities.

Botanizing time was now of greater importance to him than ever. How many more discoveries could be made in the remaining months? Near Kōnāhuanui, one of the highest tops of O'ahu at 4,000 feet, Hillebrand found one of Hawai'i's rarest and showy plants, the *Lobelia gaudichaudii*. A few of its seed were forwarded to Kew immediately. From a successful trip into the higher regions of Maui (7,000 feet), Hillebrand returned with a begonia, *Hillebrandia sandwicensis,* that he found in a long, deep mountain gorge.

In 1870, Hillebrand's ability to establish meaningful friendships once again bore fruit. When the Austrian frigate *Donau* pulled into Honolulu Harbor for major repair, Hillebrand befriended the ship's chief surgeon. Within a few days, he sent Dr. Wawra on a botanizing mission to Mount Haleakalā on Maui. Supplied by Hillebrand with an exact description of the plant and its possible location, the Austrian found the rare *Argyroxiphium* between loose lava rocks at an altitude of 8,000 to 10,000 ft. The plant's seeds, long awaited in Kew, were forwarded to England with the next ship.

In September of 1870, the illustrious Sir George Grey, British colonial governor of New Zealand, spent a few days in Honolulu on his way back home. Grey, who had developed a keen interest in Maori culture, had written a pioneering study of Maori history and mythology. He also showed a keen interest in botany. Like Hillebrand, he introduced "valuable" plants to whatever country he was assigned to. Grey spent several hours in Hillebrand's garden, seeking his host's advice in botanical matters, especially the transport of plants. The two men parted as friends. Their correspondence continued even in the late 1870s when Sir George became premier of New Zealand.

fourteen Return to the Fatherland

THE FATHERLAND OF PRUSSIA THAT Hillebrand had left behind in 1848 had undergone important changes in the last twenty years. Gone were the small principalities and kingdoms. Unified, not always peacefully, they now constituted Germany, ruled by Prussian King Wilhelm I. France had opposed the union, while England, Austria, and Russia sided with Prussia. The ensuing short, but fierce, Franco-Prussian War ended in a defeat of the French.

When Hillebrand wrote his last letter from Hawai'i to Kew in September of 1870, he had just received the breathtaking, victorious news. For the first time, he left the fine plant collection he had brought back from Maui untouched and eagerly studied the newly arrived newspapers instead. "What a glorious rising of our people against that insolent foe!" he wrote to Sir Joseph Hooker. This news made parting from

Hawai'i easier. William couldn't wait to show his wife and children his united country.

In early spring of 1871, he took leave of Kamehameha V. The king's health, still precarious but stable, was now under the care of Dr. McKibben. William had always liked Prince Lot and spent many hours in his company. He understood Lot's love and admiration for Queen Emma, a woman Hillebrand also greatly admired and respected.

When it came to the final parting from the Islands, his heart felt heavy. From the deck of the steamer, he had a last look at Diamond Head and Punchbowl, Honolulu's stern guardians. As always, clouds rested on O'ahu's silver hills, where he had discovered so many botanical secrets. He reflected on how much Honolulu had changed since his arrival twenty-one years ago. It now spread out into three directions, and thanks to his Westphalian obstinacy, his beloved trees were visible everywhere. Physically, he would be gone from these islands, but in the tradition of a good botanist, his memory would live on in his green treasures. As the coming years proved, Hawai'i always stayed close to Hillebrand's heart wherever he traveled.

• • •

The bustling port of San Francisco, California, was Hillebrand's first destination. This city had also changed since his short stay there years ago. Gone were the primitive roads and frame houses. Instead large handsome buildings lined paved streets. In the company of his San Francisco botanist friend Henry N. Bolander, Hillebrand revisited the city on the bay. Bolander, renowned collector of lichen and grasses, had just published his work, *A Catalogue of Plants Growing in the Vicinity of San Francisco*. The book was highly praised and can still be found on library shelves today.

William had decided to make use of the newly-completed transcontinental railroad line for his journey to Boston. He looked forward to the train's adventurous route through the Sierra Nevada's gold country. Virginia City, with its gold and silver mines open for investment, tempted even a prudent person like Hillebrand. Fortunes were still made at this frontier town that was bustling with thousands of residents. While checking out investment possibilities for himself and his father-in-law, Hillebrand stayed at the six-story International Hotel that overlooked, as advertised, the "richest place on earth."

During his years in Hawai'i, Hillebrand had met and befriended many Mormons. He took advantage of the stagecoach connection between Virginia City and Salt Lake City, and took up the long-standing invitation from his Mormon friends who had returned to their home state. He spent a week of gracious hospitality in Utah's fast growing city, which had a population of about 13,000 and an impressive, flourishing commerce. Well-provided for with homemade cakes by his Mormon friends, he continued his long journey to the east.

· · ·

To be a guest of Asa Gray at Harvard University was another dream come true in the life of William Hillebrand. The schoolboy of thirty years ago, who had so eagerly read and reread the natural science books in the school's library, could now claim to be friends with two of the world's most eminent botanists—Harvard's Asa Gray and Sir Joseph D. Hooker of Kew Gardens. Under the guidance of Gray, he began to assemble his huge Hawaiian collection of phanerogams and vascular cryptogams. Again, his thorough, methodical way of working became an important factor in arranging the collection.

Anna Hillebrand and her youngest son Harry had joined William in Cambridge, Massachusetts. The change of climate and a year together with her extended family on the East Coast had done wonders. Anna's physician declared her health restored. She loved the quaint streets of Cambridge with their teahouses and shops. She spent many afternoons in the stimulating company of Jane L. Gray, Asa Gray's wife. Both women had shared many botanical ventures with their husband and had plenty to talk about.

The Grays were sought-after celebrities of the botanical world. Every botanist of stature who visited the United States tried to get an invitation to the Grays. In 1871, Marianne North, English botanical painter and naturalist, arrived in Cambridge to visit them. In all probability, this well-traveled, interesting woman, who was close friends with the Hookers of Kew Gardens, met and befriended the Hillebrands during her stay. Their paths crossed again four years later, when they happened to be together on the isle of Tenerife.

Did Marianne North follow William Hillebrand's advice when she traveled to California's Sierra Nevada in 1875? After all, Mariposa Grove was Hillebrand's favorite place in the Sierra, and that is where North arrived by stagecoach with her easel. Hillebrand was well-acquainted with the proprietor and man in charge of tree logging. With his help, he had procured a slice of a big Wellington tree (*Sequoiadendron gigantum*) for Kew Gardens. It can be assumed that a letter from Hillebrand to the proprietor helped the unusual female guest to find lodgings at the grove. North painted some remarkable scenes of Mariposa Grove's giant sequoias and of nearby Yosemite Park. Together with over 800 of her watercolors and oil paintings, they grace the walls of the Marianne North Gallery at Kew Gardens.

A most productive year with Asa Gray ended for Hillebrand in May 1872. Before he left Cambridge, he sent off a quick parcel of plants to Sir Joseph D. Hooker. "Unfortunately," he wrote in his accompanying letter, "I have just found out that you will be on your way to the United States when I will take my family to Europe." This was a great disappointment for William who had looked forward to meeting his mentor, Sir Joseph D. Hooker, in person after decades of correspondence.

• • •

In the summer of 1872, the four Hillebrands boarded the steamer *India* at New York Harbor. What was supposed to be a "homecoming" for William and a new beginning for the family in quaint Heidelberg, turned into an indulgence of William's insatiable wanderlust instead. Over the next ten years, Anna, like her mother Helen Newcomb, became an expert at living out of suitcases. Both women had married husbands who relentlessly followed their passion for natural science around the globe.

Hillebrand must have felt triumphant when he arrived with his family in Hamburg, Germany. Twenty-four years ago, as a young medical doctor, he had left from this harbor to explore the world. He returned as a successful man who had achieved more than he could have dreamed of. Honored and revered in his medical profession as well as in the world of botany, he arrived in Europe financially secure and with a family he deeply loved.

He didn't choose the quickest way to Heidelberg. By railroad, he took his family from Hamburg to Bremen. There they were guests of Captain Ludwig Geerken, skipper of the *Woods*, who had been William's friend and reliable shipper of botanical goods for many years. Captain

Geerken took the Hillebrands for a visit to Bremen's green oasis, the Buerger Park (Citizen's Park). Many of the park's interesting trees were old acquaintances of William. He had sent them across the sea with Ludwig Geerken as young saplings.

Their next stop, a visit to the Baroque gardens in Herrenhausen, Hannover, delighted even the Hillebrand boys. Dr. Hermann Wendland, master gardener and longtime trading partner, gave the family a tour of the gardens with its fountains, grottos, mazes, and palm trees. Wherever Hillebrand went, he was pleased to see that despite the heavy losses that had occurred during transport and the change of habitat, the surviving plants had grown into beautiful, healthy specimens.

William was a relentless tour guide. He took his family to the cities of Braunschweig, Cologne, and Bonn before they reached Heidelberg, their final destination. For Anna Hillebrand and her eldest, William Francis, the many new impressions must have been just as overwhelming as travelling with lively 4-year-old Harry.

• • •

William was quickly accepted in the academic world of Heidelberg. As a matter of fact, he became something of a celebrity. After all, his curriculum vitae was impressive: Privy Councilor to King Kamehameha V, Minister of Immigration of the Hawaiian Islands, chief physician of Queen's Hospital in Honolulu. All doors opened to him. Anna, on the other hand, struggled to find acceptance in German female circles. After twenty years of life in the Sandwich Islands and her childhood in the young, fast-paced United States, life in Heidelberg felt like life on a different planet, a dull one at that. Anna, who had entertained Queen Emma and who had had tea with colorful, dynamic people like General Vallejo at his ranch in California, now listened patiently to small talk of the German *hausfraus*. After a few polite invitations, she soon found out that the wives of professors in Germany did not play similar roles as the ones at American universities. For many of these women, she remained the strange English-speaking woman who had lived for many years on a tropical island.

There were exceptions, of course. Professor Robert Bunsen, the famous chemist and inventor, and his wife became close friends of the Hillebrands. William Francis, by then enrolled at Heidelberg University, was one of Bunsen's chemistry students.

Henry Villard, German-American journalist, financier, and railway promoter, and close friend of president Lincoln, befriended the Hillebrands during their sojourn in Heidelberg. Both men were sons of German judges and shared the same adventurous wanderlust despite their failing health. Villard's American wife, Helen Francis Garrison Villard, daughter of anti-slavery campaigner William Garrison, felt in harmony with Anna Hillebrand. They both could look back on their interesting, not always easy lives at the side of their intrepid husbands. The Hillebrand-Villard friendship lasted for many years. William Francis Hillebrand, after his return to the United States, became a frequent visitor to the Villard's Dobbs Ferry estate in New York.

The city of Heidelberg was one of many stops in Hillebrand's journey to his fatherland.

COURTESY OF DARRELL KRAEHENBUEHL

The cold, humid winters on the shores of the Neckar River turned out to be too severe for Anna's health. In the winter of 1875, her tuberculosis returned. An inflammation of the entire upper lobe of her right lung confined her to bed for six months. Even William, despite his exciting research at the university's botanical laboratory, longed for a warmer climate. Where did well-to-do Europeans with pulmonary complaints travel in 1875?

Switzerland would have been the first choice, but Anna and William longed for island life. In the end, they decided on the isle of Madeira, 560 miles off the Moroccan coast in the Atlantic Ocean. The year-round, spring-like climate had turned tiny Madeira—thirty-five miles long, thirteen miles wide—into a health resort for tubercular patients. Mountain peaks, green valleys, and masses of flaming-red bougainvilleas hanging over precipitous basalt cliffs gave the island great beauty. A small botanical garden, not yet completed, was an added attraction for William.

In early fall of 1876, after arduous travel by train, stagecoach, and ship the Hillebrands arrived at Funchal, capitol of Madeira.

fifteen Madeira

WITH A TRAINED EYE FOR island government, Hillebrand quickly
discovered that Madeira, an integral part of Portugal, was overpopulated
and suffering from unemployment. On his daily walk through the steep
hillside vineyards, where the grapes of the famous Madeira wines
ripened in crisp sea air and sun, he watched the hardworking
Portuguese laborers tending the vineyards. Had he discovered the ideal,
much-needed immigrants for Hawai'i? He immediately wrote an excited
letter to his friend Dr. Mott-Smith in Honolulu suggesting an immigration
project to bring Portuguese laborers to Hawai'i. The reply must have been
positive because soon after, in December 1876, he followed up with an
official letter to the Hawaiian Board of Immigration. He spoke about his
favorable observations of the industriousness of the Portuguese, and the
similarity of climate and agricultural productions on Madeira. Hillebrand

foresaw no adjustment difficulties for the Portuguese laborers. He
expressed his willingness to arrange the enterprise should the Hawaiian
government so desire.

In a subsequent letter to the board, he wrote:

> In my opinion your island could not possibly
> get a more desirable class of immigrants than the
> population of the Madeira and Azores Islands. Sober,
> honest, industrious and peaceable, they combine all
> the qualities of a good settler and with all this, they
> are inured to your climate. Their education and ideas
> of comfort and social requirements are just low
> enough to make them contented with the lot of an
> isolated settler and its attendant privations, while on
> the other hand their mental capabilities and habits of
> work will ensure them much higher status in the next
> generation, as the means of improvement grow up
> around them. If the thing can be successfully initiated
> and continued, your Government ought to devote
> every dollar at its disposal to it. In saying this I start
> from the supposition that your Government intends to
> apply the appropriation made by the Legislature to
> the bona fide increase population and leave the pro-
> curement of labourers to the planters.

Hawai'i's Board of Immigration was only too happy to appoint
Hillebrand as their commissioner for the Portuguese islands. They agreed
to pay the $75 ship's passage for each adult as Hillebrand had suggested.
Agricultural employment for the first year after arrival was a guaranteed
$15 per month for the men. Hillebrand was advised to arrange ship
transport for the immigrants with the Bremen office of Honolulu's
Hackfeld & Company.

What then followed was a slow, drawn-out affair of negotiations
with the Portuguese government. Finally in November 1877, a contract
was drafted for the immigrants that stipulated a service period of thirty-
six months, with twenty-six working days per month and ten working
hours per day. Each able-bodied male was to receive $10 a month in U.S.
gold or silver and daily rations. In addition, they would have suitable

lodging, an area for a garden, medical attendance, and medicine free of charge. Working women and children were to receive smaller wages but similar prerequisites.

Portuguese laborers in Lahaina Canefield. While living in Madeira, Hillebrand recruited Portuguese contract laborers on behalf of the Hawaii Board of Immigration.

PHOTO BY RAY JEROME BAKER, 1911
COURTESY OF BISHOP MUSEUM ARCHIVES

In June 1878, when the German barque *Priscilla* arrived at Funchal Harbor, Hillebrand was there to watch the first 120 adventurous Portuguese (60 men, 22 women, and 38 children) embark on what would become one of the most successful immigration projects in Hawaiian history. Among the few worldly goods the emigrants carried onboard was the Portuguese guitar, *braguinha.* Soon it would receive the Hawaiian name *'ukulele* (lit.,"dancing fleas") and become forever synonymous with Hawaiian music worldwide. During the next ten years, seventeen ships transported 11,057 Portuguese immigrants from Madeira and the Azores to the Hawaiian Islands.

A full year of constant negotiations with the Portuguese government had given Hillebrand no time to pursue his work on *Flora of the Hawaiian Islands.* He also visited Anna daily, who was slowly recuperating in one of Funchal's sanitariums, and looked after 10-year-old Harry, who was cared for by an English governess. Meanwhile in Heidelberg, William Francis had finished his course of studies *cum laude.* This was another reason for Hillebrand to sigh with relief when the *Priscilla* left Funchal Harbor: The proud parents were now free to travel to Germany, attend William Francis' graduation, and see him off to the United States.

Henry "Harry" Thomas Hillebrand.
AUTHOR'S COLLECTION

sixteen The Air of *Freiheit* (Freedom)

ON THE DAY OF THE Festione of the Cross, May 1, 1880, a rusty potato schooner returned William Hillebrand to the harbor of Puerto Orotava on the isle of Tenerife where the family had taken up lodgings. The snow-capped mountains of the Canary Island sent a chilly breeze down its west coast, the temperature a mere 61°F.

Loaded with gifts and interesting new plants, Hillebrand arrived after a three-week stay at Las Palmas, Gran Canaria. He couldn't wait to tell his wife of his successful venture at the capital of the Canary Islands. A small announcement in Las Palmas' newspaper, which stated that he was going to hold office in April, had brought an immense patient turn-out. Many of them were wealthy Europeans who had gone out of their way to make William's stay a most pleasant one. They even tried to talk him into opening a permanent doctor's office at Las Palmas.

Financially the idea was tempting, he told Anna. But he wondered if it would be tempting enough to give up their present residence at the villa of the Marquessa de la Quinta. At an elevation of 700 feet above the sea where "the air of *freiheit* "(freedom) blew, the family had stayed for the last eighteen months. Every morning they were greeted with a breathtaking view of the celebrated Pico de Teyde, Tenerife's highest mountain.

Hillebrand liked Tenerife, preferred its climate to that of Madeira, and wondered why Europeans didn't flock here in larger numbers. Orotava's quaint botanical garden, La Hijuela del Botanico, only ten minutes walking distance from their lodgings, had been an added attraction for William. Anna, who had paid a high price to watch her eldest son receive his doctorate in Heidelberg, finally regained her health in the fresh mountain air. Whatever damage that cold, rainy summer two years ago in Germany had done to her lungs, she had forgotten now.

Anna felt better and stronger, enough so to let her husband know that the time had come to return to the European continent. She longed for friends and family. During her husband's recent absence, there had been nothing for her and Harry to do other than watch Tenerife's annual $40,000 onion crop being loaded on large vessels at Puerto Orotava's harbor.

In long letters to her eldest, William Francis, who worked as a geologist in Leadville, Colorado, Anna had poured out her longing for civilization. She described how their eccentric landlady, the Marquessa de la Quinta, had become deranged during Hillebrand's absence and left for Madrid on the spur of the moment, leaving Anna and Harry stranded at her abandoned villa above the sea. Anna had had enough. No gifts, no sweet talk could tempt her to agree to a prolonged stay at Tenerife.

Her determined words must have made William realize that his botanical pursuits had always made him feel at home wherever he went, while Anna, his loyal wife, had put up with many inconveniences over the years. There was also 13-year-old Harry's education to consider. Hillebrand had heard of Le Rosey, an excellent school recently founded in Montreux, Switzerland, which appealed to him. Switzerland it would be, William decided. He gave in to Anna's demands with one stipulation. Before leaving Tenerife, he had to solve the botanical puzzle of the *pico de paloma*, the mysterious lotus plant growing in a garden of Orotava. Was it an indigenous plant, as claimed by the shepherd who discovered it on the high cliffs to the east of the island?

When Kew Gardens confirmed two months later that *pico de paloma*

(*Lotus berthelotii*) was indeed a rare, native plant of Tenerife, Hillebrand kept his promise and began to pack his botanical collection. Overjoyed, Anna wrote to William Francis of his father's decision. Before she signed off the letter with a loving "aloha," she added a post scriptum from Hillebrand: "Please remind your colleagues in Leadville to keep their eyes open for unusual plants. Whatever they find can be dried in newspaper." When Anna pointed out to her husband that these young men were out there to make money, Hillebrand answered with his quiet sense of humor, "There must be one fool (like me) among them."

• • •

Life at the picturesque town of Montreux, on the shores of Lake Geneva, offered all William Hillebrand had promised his wife: grand mountains that protected the lakeside community from icy north and east winds, elegant hotels, cultural events, and medieval castles. Montreux's balmy climate, in which palm trees and exotic flowers thrived year-round, attracted interesting and colorful people from all over the world. Russian royalty, famous composers, musicians, and dancers—Anna could observe them all on her afternoon strolls on the promenade.

Harry had been accepted at the prestigious Le Rosey School for Boys, and William could finally settle down and complete his *Flora of the Hawaiian Islands*. Setbacks like the loss of a package of mosses and a part of his manuscript, which he had sent to General Munro at Kew Gardens for evaluation, brought temporary excitement to his life. His distress mounted when he heard that the old general had passed away. Five months later, Munro's executor found the package in the deceased's estate. William breathed easier.

The years 1881 to 1884 at the Maison Lonney in Montreux were possibly the happiest years the Hillebrands had since their departure from Hawai'i. Their new domicile at this ideal location brought on the visits of many of their friends and relatives from overseas. John Mott-Smith, now the Hawaiian Commissioner in Washington, came for a visit with his wife. In 1883, an invitation went out to botany's great Asa Gray of Harvard and his wife Jane. The Hillebrands were looking forward to repaying the Grays' hospitality of 1872.

Hillebrand's affiliation with Hawai'i and its causes continued strong. His article, "The Contagium of Leprosy," appeared in European

and American medical journals as well as in the *Pacific Commercial
Advertiser.* In the spring of 1883, Edward Christian Arning, a young
German dermatologist specializing in leprosy, visited Hillebrand in
Montreux. Arning, who had received a grant from the Humboldt
Institute of the Royal Prussian Academy of Science for a study tour of
leprosy in Hawai'i and the acquisition of an ethnographic collection,
begged Hillebrand to help him obtain the approval of the proper
Hawaiian authorities. Through his close ties to Walter Murray Gibson, then
minister of foreign affairs, Hillebrand was able not only to assure Arning
acceptance from Hawai'i's medical community, but also the promise of a
monthly salary of $150. Hillebrand was happy to have been able to oblige
the young doctor, but as it turned out, Arning became a controversial,
difficult man. Scholarly and stubborn, he fought small wars with Walter
Murray Gibson until his services were terminated in 1886. Complaints
Hillebrand received from Arning, as well as from his former Hawaiian
medical colleagues, proved a deep disappointment.

Whatever time William devoted to his
guests or Montreux's cultural diversions,
he made up with nighttime work on his
Flora of the Hawaiian Islands. By Christmas
of 1884, the manuscript had grown to 700
pages with at least 100 more to go. William
realized that had he remained in Germany, the
project would be finished by now. His wanderlust, fueled by the excuse of Anna's illness, had
cost him valuable time.

In the winter of 1884, it was Anna's turn
to keep a wary eye on her husband. William,
who had always been on the slim side, had lost
considerable weight. He looked gaunt and his
once-black hair had turned icy gray. He
appeared to be in pain. When he discontinued
his daily shoreline walks at Geneva's Lac
Leman, which he had enjoyed so much,
Anna knew something was seriously wrong.

"What will the new year have in
store for Papa?" she worried in her Christmas
letter to William Francis in Colorado.

Excerpts from Hillebrand's original manuscript,
Flora of the Hawaiian Islands. *It was published
posthumously in 1888 and was the most authori-
tative reference on Hawaiian plants for the next
century. The original manuscript was given to the
Bishop Museum in 1929.*

seventeen A Journey's End

ONCE AGAIN, THE HUGE WICKER trunks that had accompanied the Hillebrands from Hawai'i to Asia and on to Europe arrived in Heidelberg. This time, in the summer of 1885, they were delivered to the imposing two-story sandstone building at Bergheimer Strasse 18. A shiny brass nameplate on the right side of the entrance stated that Privy Councillor Dr. William Hillebrand resided there.

This was the time of the year when the golden summer sun would shine on the ruins of the Heidelberg castle and onto the hills that rose up the sides of the glistening Neckar River. The city's narrow streets were filled with young students who had come to Heidelberg to begin their fall semester, like Hillebrand did forty years ago.

The Hillebrands had returned to the city where their European sojourn began fourteen years before. No doubt, William's enthusiasm then had turned into a more solemn mood in 1885. The new lodgings, in walking distance to the Akademische Hospital, were chosen wisely by William. Constantly in pain, he must have known that he would soon be in need of good medical care. His illness, although described in letters as "excruciably" painful, didn't seem to be life threatening. Unfortunately, a proper diagnosis does not appear in any of the letters currently available.

Heidelberg proved to be a stepping-stone in William and Anna's return to the United States. Anna longed to be together with her eldest son, William Francis, and her family in New York. She had already seen more than half of the world, was tired of living out of suitcases, and wanted to have a permanent home. Her 18-year-old son Harry graduated from Le Rosey in Switzerland and was ready to enter college. William decided it was time for the family to join their eldest in the United States.

But there was his life's work, the yet unfinished *Flora of the Hawaiian Islands*. With the assistance of his Heidelberg friend and botanist, Professor Eugen Askenasy, the manuscript would be ready for publication in a few months time. However, the first contacts with German publishers were disappointing. The book, written in English and for a small, select group, did not entice any of the publishing houses that were approached. William resigned himself to the fact that he would have to publish the book at his own expense. Still, there was a slim hope that the Hawaiian government would aide him with a grant. After all, the book was designed to be useful not only to botanists, but also to amateur Hawaiian nature-lovers who were interested in their native flora. William remembered them well, the men and women of his volunteer workforce who had spent many hours collecting native plants for him. For these friends, he intended to include a basic outline of botany as an aid for a better understanding of the science. Until the manuscript was finished and the publishing problems solved, he had to remain in Germany.

William thought it was time to get his affairs in order. Urgent letters crossed the Atlantic, asking his son William Francis if he would be willing to take care of his mother and younger brother until his father could join them. William Francis, a former chemist at the Denver branch of the United States Geological Survey, had recently been transferred to the head office in Washington. Once William and Anna were assured that their eldest would take care of his mother and brother, travel arrangements were made for Anna and Harry to join William Francis in Washington.

From Berlin came the news that Henry Villard, Hillebrand's friend who was known as the "United States railroad king," had taken up residence at Germany's metropolis. For William this must have been exciting news and another reason to pack his suitcase once again. He combined a long-standing visit to the Berlin Imperial Museum of Natural Sciences with a visit to the Villards. After all, William had decided to leave his entire plant collection to the Imperial Museum once his book was finished. (Unfortunately, this collection was destroyed by Allied bombs during World War II.)

Berlin, capitol of the new German empire, had become one of the most interesting cities in culture, arts, and science in Europe. This was a German city that even Anna liked. Anna and William looked forward to meeting Henry and Fanny Villard again. At Henry Villard's house, the high and mighty of European arts and politics met. Modest William was not beyond enjoying their elegant dinner parties in the company of Germany's glitterati.

This most enjoyable visit to Berlin was Anna and William Hillebrand's last journey together. In late fall of 1885, Anna and Harry traveled to Hamburg where they boarded a steamer to the United States. Anna had her husband's promise to join the family in Washington by early summer 1886. But it was the one promise William Hillebrand couldn't keep.

•   •   •

On July 14, 1886, when the Heidelberg burghers opened their morning paper, they saw the black-bordered, 3x4 inch notice that announced the death of Dr. William Hillebrand. In the note, professor Eugen Askenasy let friends and acquaintances know that the esteemed doctor had died at the Akademische Hospital the previous day at 11 A.M. Funeral arrangements were set for Thursday the fifteenth and the funeral procession would leave from the Akademische Hospital at 4 P.M. on that day.

It was at this time of the year, July 1886, that the Neckar Valley—known for its sultry and humid summer weather—had shown extreme low barometric pressure. Low hanging clouds and partly heavy rains caused a most unhealthy climate for people who suffered from a heart or pulmonary condition. William Hillebrand died on such a day, July 13. William Francis later wrote in the foreword to *Flora of the Hawaiian Islands* that his father had died a sudden death. It can be assumed that the climate was a contributing factor in William Hillebrand's demise.

An ad taken out by Eugen Askenasy in the Heidelberg newspaper announced the death of Dr. William Hillebrand.

At 4 P.M. on Thursday, July 15, a horse-drawn hearse bearing Hillebrand's casket left the Akademische Hospital. Despite a driving rain, many of Hillebrand's friends and colleagues gathered to accompany their respected friend on his last journey to the hillside cemetery of Bergfriedhof. The cemetery was famous for its beautiful view over the Rhine Valley and its incorporation of a well-designed horticultural layout. The Bergfriedhof was a fitting resting place for Hillebrand, a man who had dedicated a great part of his life to the science of botany.

Thanks to his vision and deep love for Hawai'i, the Islands' agriculture prospered and the beauty of Hawaiian flora became known worldwide. In the heart of Honolulu, Hillebrands' green oasis, Foster Botanical Gardens, lives on and thrives as a monument to Dr. William Hillebrand's love and devotion for the Hawaiian Islands and their people.

Appendix

Letters from Hillebrand to Kew Gardens, 1857–1881

These letters can be found at the archives of the Royal Botanical Gardens at Kew, London. Variances in spelling and punctuation have been left as they appear in the original letters. Any comments/additions by the author are enclosed in brackets [ ].

[Director's correspondence vol. 71, ff. 133]

Sir W. J. Hooker
May 20, 1857
Sir

Some time ago H.B.M. Consul-General Wm. Miller, Esq. handed to me a communication from you of March 8, [18]56 to G.L. Conyngham Esq. reletive [sic] to the <u>Kalo</u> and other plants, belonging to our islands. Happy, to be offered an opportunity to do service to a man of such scientific eminence, I gladly acceded to the request of General Miller to forward the plants desired by you.

Accordingly I have made up a box, which will leave tomorrow by the barque Yankee under charge of Dr. F. Hutchison for England via Panama containing

3 or 4 plants of the <u>awa</u> *Macropiper methisticum*

6 dz. of the <u>Ti</u> *Dracaena terminalis*

10–12 dz of the <u>kalo</u> *Caladium esculentum*

10–12 dz of the <u>apé</u> – not an arum, as the Forsters thought, but a *Gunnera*, according to my friend Jules Remy, who has seen it in flower.

12 tubers (resembling the potato) of the <u>pia</u>- *Tacca pinnatifida*

2 suckers of the <u>wauke</u> *Boehmeria alba*, of the fiber of which tree the natives prepare their <u>Kapa</u> [illegible]

Besides these you will receive in a package seeds

1. of an undescribed palm, about 10 ft. high with flabelli form leaves, called <u>Loulu</u> by the natives, who eat its nuts. Its elevation is from the seashore to 3000 ft.

2. of an arborescent Asparaginea – <u>Halapepe</u>, of the soft wood of which the natives used to carve their idols 20–30 ft. high, elev. 800–2000 ft. Gaudichaud, I believe erroneously, took it for a Pandanea and called it *Freycinetia arborea*.

   Mr. J. Remy has described both accurately and con- siders them to be [illegible] each a new genus—the former of which he intends to dedicate to me and the other to our common friend J. L. Brenchley.

3. of a new arborescent *Hibiscus* with large yellow flowers, which I found in an old lava field on East Maui.

4. of the *Sida ulmifolia*

5. of the <u>Sandal</u> — *Santalum album*.The seeds of this are only few in number and I cannot vouch for their being well matured. But in a short time I shall be able to send more.

Dr. Hutchison has kindly offered to take the best care of them during the transit.

You expressed in your communication the opinion, that the <u>Kalo</u> would keep well for a long time, so that it might be transported in vessels doubling Cape Horn. Such however is not the case, it seldom keeps longer than four weeks, even when raised on dry land, as is done at higher elevations. This vegetable is cultivated up to a height of 4000 ft, but is most prolific when raised in the lower regions, under water. The water has, however, to be renewed at least twice a week. In stagnant, decomposing water it rots quickly, as was the case in many localities during the great drought of last summer.

I had collected several other plants of economical use which I intended to transmit to you: amongst them 3 kinds of fern with edible roots; 1 *Dioscoroea* and one *Tamus*[1] with very large tubers, both serving as food for the natives, and of which the former particularly is very palatable; the <u>olona</u> yielding a kind of substitute for the hemp fiber and others, but want of room in the box has obliged me to lay them aside until an opportunity offers of sending them by a man of war.

With regard to the <u>awa</u> I will here remark, that its reputed anti-syphilitic property seems to me rather doubtful, but its usefulness against old rheumatic and gouty complaints is incontestable.

If you should deem it desirable to avail yourself of my services for the future in procuring seeds or plants of our islands for the Kew Gardens, I have only to state that I shall take the greatest pleasure in furthering your views and thereby contributing my share to the advancement of science. My position as resident medical practitioner in Honolulu for the last 6 years and my acquaintance with the flora of the group affords me great facilities for this purpose.

Besides, I may mention, that I have domiciled in my private garden many of the most remarkable plants and trees of our islands and that I am going to follow the same plan on a larger scale in a nursery garden, which our Agricultural Society has just begun to establish and of which the general management will probably devolve on me.

Speaking of these gardens, I credit myself of this opportunity to solicit your kind patronage in the promotion of our laudable efforts, to

---

[1] Could be *"Pamur"* or *"Famus,"* none of which makes sense.

introduce in our little kingdom as many of the useful and beautiful productions of our nature as we possibly can. For particular in a few classes of
plants we are most desirous of introducing, I will mention

1. all tropical fruit trees (we possess only the banana, Tamarind,
    Ohai *(Jambosa malacc[ense])* Papaya, Guyava, mango, custard
    apple (anona), avocado pear *(Persea grat[issima])*. The mangosteen
    before all others we are anxious to introduce.
2. the different cereals and useful pasture grasses of the tropics
    and subtropical countries. (Of the former we posses the
    maize, Durra *(Sorg[hum] Vulg[are])* and *Sorg. Sacchar[atum])*
3. all kinds of spice-trees and plants, as the clove, cinnamon,
    nutmeg, cardamom, Star anise, Pimento, pepper, etc. (Only
    ginger and capsicum have been introduced hitherto). I will
    mention here also the camphor trees, both of Japan and Sumatra.
4. Palm trees of every description.
5. Forest and shade trees, particularly such as yield a good timber,
    as the *Hymenaea Courbaril, Bertholetia excelsa,* the teak tree. I will
    also mention the Gutta Percha tree.
6. Any fine flowering shrubs or trees, viz. the *Amherstia, Ionesia,*[2]
    Mesua, Barringtonia, etc.
7. Some representatives of the beautiful families of Orchidacea
    and Scitamineae. Of the former we have none and of the latter
    only 2 native species, a *Zingiber* and a *Curcuma.*

If you should feel inclined to second our endeavor we do not
wish you to confine yourself to the foregoing list, which merely points
out some classes of vegetable that have mostly attracted our attention.
Whatever you could send us from the tropics and subtropics—our
highlands enjoy a very cool climate—particularly from Africa, the East
and West Indies, Guiana, Brasil, countries with which we do not have
communication whatever, would be most acceptable. With Australia and
several parts of the West Coast of America I have opened already a direct
correspondence. Perhaps you could recommend us to the kind attention
of the botanical gardens in Calcutta from which port frequently vessels
go to San Francisco or to some friend of botany or agriculture in
Jamaica and Demerara, from which places seeds may quickly arrive by
the steamers via Panama and San Francisco.

I have requested Mr. Hutchison to call shortly before his return
to the Islands at your residence at the Kew Gardens to take charge of

---

[2] This word is problematic; it could be *"Jonesia,"* or even *"Garcinia."*

anything you might be pleased to send us for our gardens: He intends to leave England some time in September or October.

Please, Sir, to inform me soon of the condition in which the plants have arrived and accept the expression of the highest respect from your most obedient
Wm. Hillebrand MD

P.S. I take the liberty to transmit to you a few numbers of the transactions of the R. H. Agricultural Soc. for which I am presently acting as Corresp. Secretary.

[Director's correspondence vol. 71, ff. 134]

Honolulu June 23, 1857
Sir W. J. Hooker
Sir,
By the present I send you seeds of

1. *Santalum album*
2. *Edwardsia chrysophylla* elev. 1800–2500 ft.
3. Some dry heads of the *Argyrophyton Douglasii* which were sent to me recently from East Maui where it grows on the mountain Haleakala at an elevation of about 8000 ft. The seeds are seldom found perfect, as a certain insect, attracted by a glutinous substance exuded by the plant, almost invariably destroys them.
4. Some seed capsules of a tree, growing at the western end of Oahu at the foot of the mountains. I have not had occasion to see the tree myself, but it is said, to shed its leaves in summer.

Please to accept the expression of highest respect from Your most humble servant
Wm Hillebrand, MD

[*Director's Correspondence vol. 71, ff. 135*]

Honolulu Sept 18, 1857
Sir W. J. Hooker
Sir,

Only late last evening I was informed by Gen. Miller that the ship "Kamehameha IV" is to sail this day at noon for England. I regret very much not to have received this intelligence earlier, as it would have afforded me a good opportunity to send a box with plants, but which cannot be done on so short a notice, as I have to procure the plants from the hills. I have, however, found time to make up a package with the following seeds:

1. *Sequoia gigantea* from California
2. of a large tree from the Marquesas called by the natives there Koai
3. a *Casuarina* from the Marquesas Isl.
4. *Acacia heterophylla* (called Koa by the natives). This tree, which grows to the height of 30 or 40 ft is one of the most ornamental trees of our group, and now becoming of great commercial importance, as its wood is much esteemed by cabinetmakers, being capable to assume a fine polish, not inferior to Mahogany. Its bark is used for tanning.
5. *Calophyllum inophyllum*. Its wood is likewise much esteemed for cabinet work.
6. *Santalum Freycinetianum*
7. Naau,[3] a tree of which I only found the fruit. The pulp in which the seeds nodulate, used formerly to be employed as a dye for their Kapa by the natives. It is rare.

6 and 7. 2 species of *Scaevola*

8. *Petesia terminalis*
9. another Rubiacea
10. *Cyathodes Kameiameiae*
11. an Oleinea, called Maile, shrubby
12. *Dianella*
13. *Verbesina*
14. *Solanum*

In a former letter I said, in speaking of the Apé, that I had been informed by Mr. Remy that it was a *Gunnera*. Since however I have seen it in flower and convinced myself, that it is an Aroidea—a *Caladium* so far as I would judge.

---

[3] The spelling Naau is clear. This must refer to Nanu (*Gardenia* spp.), which in the *Flora* (pp. 171–172) Hillebrand says "pulp of the fruit was employed for dying <<kappa>> yellow."

If you should be pleased, to forward any seeds for our gardens from Kew or cause to be sent from the English Colonies, I would beg you to direct the same to my father in law Dr. Wesl. Newcomb in Albany, state N. York, who will send them on by express via Panama, as soon as received.

For the transmission of seeds, coming from Calcutta or other parts of the East Indies, Sir I. Bowring in Hong Kong has kindly offered his services. What we most desire from that quarter is the Mangosteen, and the different spice trees and plants.

Hoping, that I may succeed in course of time to represent our Island Group worthily at the Royal Gardens of Kew

I remain, Sir, with my greatest respect, your very humble & obdt. [obedient] servant

Wm Hillebrand, MD

[*Director's correspondence vol. 71, ff. 136*]

Honolulu Febr. 23, 1858
Sir W. J. Hooker
My dear Sir,

Your most obliging letters of Sept. 1 and Nov. 29 were duly received by me and have caused me the greatest pleasure. I should have answered your first letter instantly if on the day of its arrival I had not been informed that Dr. Hutchinson would return to Honolulu by the next packet. He arrived a fortnight ago and brought me that beautiful collection of plants you had made up for him. I can hardly tell you how much pleasure you have caused me by sending them. The greatest part were apparently in good condition and I indulge the hope, to raise at least three fourths of the Orchideae, perhaps all of them. Only two plants had completely perished, the *Boehmeria nivea* and the *Isoloma Deraiiniana*.[4] The Gloxinias and *Achimenes* looked quite fresh, but the *Chrysanthemum* rather doubtful. By sending the Cochineal insect and plant you have wonderfully anticipated my wishes, for I do not recollect to have written to you about them. During the last year and a half I have made three ineffectual attempts to procure the insect from Guatimala [*sic*], Acapulco and Panama; the people in those countries [illegible], they have a right to keep God's blessing for themselves and therefore do their best to prevent other people from getting them. I knew indeed, that the insect was reared in the Apothecaries Garden at Chelsea, but it never occurred to me, that it was so easy to transmit the same. Of the three joints of *Opuntia* you sent, two were completely dead, but one arrived healthy. Until now, I am sorry to say, I have not been able to find a living creature issue from the cottony web, which adheres to the joint, however, I have not given my hope up yet and examine every morning carefully with eye and magnifier. But even if this attempt should fail, I certainly think the insect may be sent and live another time, particularly if it should make the passage in summer. I expect important results from the introduction of the insect into our islands, where large tracts of arid sandy soil are thickly covered already by the *Opuntia tuna*. Besides there are two other kinds of *Opuntia* here, one of which I suspect to be the <u>Cochinillifera</u>.

I am really sorry to hear, that the contents of the box Dr. Hutchinson took with him, arrived in so bad a condition. It might have been foreseen indeed, for the difficulties attending a passage over the Isthmus are too great. However, what has failed in the beginning may succeed at the end.

---

[4] An unpublished name; it appears neither in the *Index Kewensis,* nor in the IPNI on-line name list. *Isoloma* is a genus of Gesneriaceae.

Since my letter of May 20 I have written you once again and have handed to General Miller three times small packages of seeds, amongst which were good ripe seeds of *Santalum*, of an interesting spiny new …thoxylon,[5] of the beautiful *Argyrophyton Douglasii* (there are two species of *Argyroph.* on Mauna Haleakala in Maui, one with white silky and the other with green leaves) and of another beautiful tree, of which the seed was sent to me from the East end of Oahu, but which has not been seen by me in flower. You will probably have received them before this, although I was not a little chagrined to see, when I called on the General one day about the beginning of January, that he was just handing over to a captain of a merchant vessel the seeds I gave him in September. It is likely enough, that most of them have lost their germinating power before coming into your hands. For the future I shall take care myself of the forwarding of seeds. Now allow me to make a few statements and inquiries regarding some of your remarks about plants.

1. The <u>Apé</u> I have had in flower in my garden last summer and found to be unmistakably an Aroidea—a *Caladium*, I should think. Its flowers possesses a strong sickly fragrance. I am at a loss to see how Remy should have mentioned it to me as a *Gunnera*—a genus of plants which was then unknown to me. It bears the marks of an Aroidea so evidently on its face, that I am rather inclined to attribute the mistake to a *lapsus linguae* on his—or a misunderstanding on my part. I do not see by your letter if it arrived sound.

2. the <u>Awa</u> Do you possess it in England?

3. the <u>Loulu</u> palm is undoubtedly indigenous. It grows on all islands and principally on almost inaccessible mountain crags, called palis by the natives, at an elevation of 2 or 3000 ft, with exception of the islands Molokai, where it touches the seashore. It grows to the height of 20 ft, has fan shaped leaves and edible fruit or nuts. Of the leaves the natives make hats and fans. I have seen only one bunch of flower 3 years ago, but I shall dry flowers as well as small fruit for you. Gaudichaud has seen the tree, but not in flower.

4. <u>Halapepe</u>. That this be Gaudichaud's *Freycinetia arborea* I have said again on the authority of Mr. Remy; if right or wrong, I cannot determine. The tree is certainly an Asparaginea, as perhaps you may have convinced yourself after examining the

[5] The first letters are illegible. No name checked in the *Flora* index matches the final letters of this name.

seed. It seems to me to be a *Dracaena*, or at all events to stand near it: the peduncles are articulated. Has Gaudichaud described a *Freycinetia arborea* as occurring on the Sandwich Islands? I have never seen or heard of a *Freycinetia* here, but of the *Fr. scandens* and the Halapepe is hardly ever found, unless it be in the embraces of this graceful climber. The leaves of both resemble each other greatly, when seen at a height (the Halapepe grows to 40 ft and more) although those of the latter have smooth margins and are not arranged in spiral volutions. I must own, that when I saw the tree first, mingled with the *Fr. scandens* I took it for a Pandanea. If Gaud. has enumerated his *Fr. arborea* amongst the representatives of the Hawaiian flora, I should not be surprised to learn that he has committed the indiscretion of setting the Halapepe down as such, of which he probably saw neither flower nor fruit and perhaps even the leaves only at a considerable height. I must remark here, that Remy before his departure from France had the privilege of examining Gaudichaud's manuscripts. I shall send you good specimens as soon as obtainable.

5. The Oloná is our best fibre plant. I have not had occasion to examine it in flower, but it is an Urticacea, probably a *Procris*.

6. The Koa is the *Acacia Heterophylla*. Its wood is capable of a splendid polish. It and the Kamani (*Caloph. inoph.*) are our best timber trees. I have charged a cabinetmaker here to save pieces of the different kind of native woods, as they come to his hand, which I shall transmit to you in due time.

7. Enclosed in this letter you find a hairy or fibrous substance called "Pulu," the product of a fern, a sample of which is added. The Pulu forms at present an important article of export from these islands to California, where it is used for stuffing mattresses and cushions. From 150 to 300,000 pounds have been sent to San Francisco annually for the four or five last years. It sells there at from 10 to 20 cents per pound. I take the fern to be the *Cibotium glaucum* Kaulf. Am I right? It is arborescent and has large tripinnate fronds.

8. I include 2 other specimens of a plant, the determination of which has puzzled me. Its habit is that of an Ericacea, but its analysis leads me to Ardisiads,[6] and yet it does not agree

---

[6] The spelling is correct; the name seems to refer to *Ardisia* (Myrsinaceae) or something closely related.

exactly with them. I found the plant only in one place on the pali of Kalihi valley, which is of most difficult access—and hardly has been visited by other white men. It stands in company with our native *Vaccinium* at about 2000 ft. I shall send you more complete specimens at a later time. It is a shrub 6 ft. high.

With regard to dried specimens for your herbarium, I here promise you to send you duplicates of all my collected plants, and they shall be perfect specimens. But I regret to say that my present collection is not very ample, all the results of my rambles over the islands of Kauai and Maui (in '54 and '55) having been destroyed by insects. I now drag every specimen with corrosive sublimate, before laying it aside. Still, I think, I have several now which have not been described yet or seen in flower by any botanist. You are kind enough to hold out to me the flattering prospect of furnishing the material for a flora insul. Sandw. I should at once take hold of the delightful project with hand and heart, if I did not entertain some scruples with regard to my friend Remy. He has resided 4 years on these islands—and visited nearly every corner of them. I think almost the Sandw. Isl. province belongs legitimately to him. And yet, I fear from his migratory tendencies and easy habits, that the scientific world will have to wait a considerable time before it learns the result of his labors. I will not dismiss the subject for the present; you will receive from me all the necessary material and after communication with Mr. Remy we may see what is best to do. A current compendium of our Island flora in the English language would be of great use here on the spot, where there are a good many young fellows who would devote themselves to the delightful study of Botany, if they only had a guide to direct them. I myself have felt the want of it sorely, and if I not had the good luck to get hold of your work on the plants collected on Beecheys Expedition, I do not know how I should have got along. What I have said here, shall however not prevent you from describing any new plants you may find amongst those I shall send. The ferns in particular I consider so much your property that I think no one else ought to meddle with them.

In May next my father in law Dr. W. Newcomb, at present residing in Albany, N.Y., is going to visit his conchological friend H. Cummings in London. I shall try to send him seeds and if possible plants also before he leaves, to deliver to you in London. It frequently occurs, that acquaintances of mine make the trip over the isthmus from here, and they are in general quite ready to charge themselves with small packages. If you would name me any friend of yours in N. York to whom they might be delivered there, I could in general manage to send you seeds as fresh as possible. If Dr. Newcomb comes, he will hold his hands open to receive anything you may have to give to him for my garden, and I doubt, if he will make it a condition "that the package must be small indeed." If you also could give him a few more Cochineal insects the chance would be greatly better for their safe arrival here, than it was the last time, as they would make the passage in the summer months.

I must not forget here to mention, that I have placed a glass case on board the Missionary schooner "Morning Star," which every year makes a trip from here to the Amer. Mission. stations in the Marquesas— and another to those in the Caroline, Kingsmith and Redark Groups. I have sent circulars to the Missionaries there, to urge them to forward living plants and seeds. – Perhaps I may be able for the future to render you some service from that quarter. With Melbourne and Sidney I have already established exchanges, and upon your advice I have also written to Dr. Thompson in Calcutta. Our Agricultural Society has acquired fifty acres of fine land in Nuuanu Valley, 2-1/2 miles from Honolulu, at an elevation of 600 ft above the sea. As the management of it has devolved on me, I have just begun to domiciliate in it some of the useful and interesting plants of our island flora. I cherish the idea that it may in time become a useful institution. Could you send us seeds of the *Cassia lanceolata, Acacia nilotica, arabica* or *seyal*? These and many other officinal plants would find here a suitable climate. I will name also the different species of *Pistacia*.

Perhaps it will interest you to hear, that during the last year we have introduced here the honeybee, which prospers remarkably well, two pairs of deer (elk) from California, a lot of terrapins and last, not least, a squad of frogs whose delightful music, I trust, will add not a little to the amenity of our charming moonlight nights.

Hoping, dear Sir, to hear from you again soon, I remain your most obedient and faithful
Wm. Hillebrand

[Director's correspondence vol. 71, ff. 137]

Honolulu April 30, 1858
Sir W. J. Hooker
Dear Sir,

As I received four days ago a small parcel of seeds from a friend, collected by him during an ascent of Mauna Haleakala on East Maui, amongst which are sound seeds of the *Argyrophytum Douglasii* one of our most interesting plants I avail myself of the opportunity offered by the departure of a gentleman from these islands, Mr. Archer, for England, to transmit you the same without delay. I send them just as I received them, of course without names, excepting the *Argyroph.* and *Santalum.* The <u>Pilo</u> is a Rubiaceous shrub only growing on the highest mountains from 4–8000 ft elevation. Have the species of *Fragaria, Vaccinium, Rubus* and *Ranunculus,* belonging to our mountain flora, been determined by any botanist?

In haste,
Your most respectfully
Wm Hillebrand

[Director's correspondence vol. 75, ff. 81]

Honolulu, Sept. 15, [18]58
Sir Wm. J. Hooker
Dear Sir,

With the present I send you a collection of seeds which I made during a recent trip to the highlands of East Maui and during an excursion of the old volcano Haleakala (house of the sun). It comprises a good many peculiar to our mountain flora. In particular I will call your attention to our mountain raspberry which bears a fruit which, for size and juiciness I have not seen paralleled. A little more sweetness added to its succulency would make it a first rate fruit, and I trust, that this result may be attained by cultivation in the hands of experienced gardeners.

The strawberry also is a great favorite with the inhabitants of those regions. I consider myself lucky to have found seeds of our rare Compositae (two species of *Dubautia*) a *Tetramapolium* [sphalm *Tetramalopium*] and what I take to be the *Aster subulatus*. One *Dubautia* is beautiful when in full bloom. I have enriched my collection of dried plants considerably, particularly in ferns, of all of which I shall transmit you specimens before next spring. I sent a package of seeds by Dr. Newcomb, which must have come to your hands before this.

Hoping to hear from you soon, I remain with my greatest respects Your most obdt. [obedient] svt. [servant]
Wm. Hillebrand

P.S. Will you please to inform me in what paper or books Gaudichaud's descriptions have been published? W. H.

[Director's correspondence vol. 75, ff. 82]

Honolulu March 27, 1859
Sir W. J. Hooker
Dear Sir,

With the present I send you another small parcel of seeds, which I have an opportunity of forwarding by an overland passenger to New York. Another larger parcel I sent about two months ago which has been delivered in San Francisco to one of the American Express Companies. The same must be in your hands before this. Whenever you find it convenient to make up for me a package with bulbs, tubers and seeds, I would request you, to forward it to the care of R. C. Janion, Esq., Hawaiian Consul in Liverpool, who possesses facilities for transmitting small packages overland at reduced rates. It would be advisable to use the lightest, least bulky material for packaging as far as it will not interfere with the safety of the plants. Orchids, Zingiberacea, Liliacea, and congeners I take the liberty to recommend to your special consideration. Of seeds I should like to have those of the different species of Pistacia, of the Carob tree, of the Argan tree,[7] and such Coniferae as will thrive in a warm country.

The garden of our Agric. Society comprising about 30 acres of fine arable soil in Nuuanu Valley and is already issuing a handsome appearance, although the first soil was turned over only a year ago. I hope it will do as much for the furtherance of botanical science as it certainly must do for the fruitful expansions of the resources of this country. I feel confident, that I need only to mention it, in order to recommend this nascent institution to your favor and patronage.

Believe me, Sir, that whatever you will do by increasing the number of its vegetable treasures, will be most gratefully acknowledged by our whole community, but in especial by your devoted and obdt. [obedient] svt. [servant]
Wm. Hillebrand

---

[7] Argan tree is *Argania* (SPT), which has a variety of economic uses.

[Director's correspondence vol. 75, ff. 83]

Honolulu Decemb. 14, 1861
Sir W. J. Hooker
Dear Sir,

   At last, after many delays I have been enabled to redeem my promise
to send you dried specimens of plants of our islands. As you will see by the
enclosed receipt, I have sent by the Bremen whaleship "Republic" a box containing about 110 numbers of ferns and Lycopodiaceae and a suite of our
Urticaceae, to be delivered to Mr. Ludwig Geerken in Bremen and to be kept
by that gentleman, subject to your orders. You will do well, immediately after
receipt of these lines to write to Mr. L. Geerken and to give him directions
how to transmit the case to its destination. The present remittance you must
consider only as a first installment, which shall be followed by others in the
measure. As I proceed with the arrangement of my herbarium or make new
additions to the plants already collected, until you are in possession of our
entire flora as far as it will be in my power to gather it. After this shall have
been accomplished I wish you would take measures to have a flora of the
Hawaiian Archipelago elaborated and published if possible by yourself or your
son Dr. Jos. Hooker. If I had the assurance that the work would be done I
should take extraordinary pains to complete the material. Already now I have
reason to believe that my collection is richer than any single one made here
before although it does not include the islands of Kauai and Hawaii yet. But as
I have recently succeeded in interesting a few young friends of the Punahou
College in the study of botany—young fellows with sound lungs and limber
legs—who will without great difficulty ascend our highest peaks and steepest
rocks and crags, I strongly hope, that before another year is out, there will be
very few lacunae left in my herbarium.

   The suite of ferns which I have sent you does not include all the
species in my possession, of some I have only a single specimen, and these I
have for the present deemed it inexpedient to part with, as by so doing I
should have deprived myself of all means of comparison for the future. They
will however all reach you finally.

   In a former letter I expressed some scruples at your suggestion about
a flora of these islands, out of regard for the labour of Mr Jules Remy, who left
the islands in 1855, but accounts since received from France leave me little
hope that the work will be done in that quarter.

   I have sent the Urticaceae this time, because this order contains some
plants of economical importance. In particular, I should like to hear your

opinion in regard to the value of the fibre of the <u>Oloná</u>, of which you will find two samples, one crude and the other prepared as twine, in the box. This fibre is used by the natives exclusively for the manufacture of their fishing nets and seines, on account of its strength and durability. Specimens of the plant with male and female flowers you will find under No. 7 of the Urticaceae. It would seem to me to be an *Elatostemma*. It only grows in damp gulches and deep recesses of our valleys, particularly in some districts of East Maui and Hawaii. I have engaged Mr. Wyllie, the King's Minister of For. Affairs, to include a fishing net made of <u>Oloná</u> amongst the articles to be sent to the World's Fair in London.

Another question I should like to have you answer me, you are aware that in former times our natives used to prepare their cloth from various species of *Procris* (<u>mamake</u>), *Neraudia* (<u>maaloa</u>), *Broussonetia* (<u>wauke</u>), and *Urtica*. I do not know, to what extent the cultivation of any plant could enter into competition with the rag trade of Continental Europe for the purpose of papermaking, but as two of those plants, the *Procris alba* and *Broussonetia* grow here in great abundance and could, without great labor or expense be multiplied almost indefinitely, I should gladly see them turned to some account for increasing the prosperity of this country. You will find a sample of <u>wauke kapa</u> with the plants; so also of <u>pulu</u>. The product of *Cibotium menziesii* which is shipped in great quantities to California and Oregon, where it is used for stuffing pillows and mattresses. I have lately found it useful also as a haemostyptic, externally applied, a property which since, I had the gratification to read, is also predicated of the kindred product of the Baranetz.[8] Are you aware what a fine cabinet wood our <u>Koa</u> yields (*Acacia heterophylla, Acacia Koa* of Asa Gray)? To my taste it makes handsomer furniture than mahogany. Only the cabinetmakers say it is hard to work into veneers. An equally esteemed cabinet wood is yielded by the <u>Kamani</u> (*Calophyllum inoph.*) of which the supply is however very limited.

The package of seeds and plants which you had the kindness to send me per "Grecian" last year, arrived in good condition considering the length of the voyage—6 months. The bulbs and rhizomes of the *Amaryllis, Methonicas,*[9] *Zingiber, Curcuma,* most *Achimenes* and several other Gesneriaceae have come out well, but that fine set of *Caladium bicolor,* the *Calathea* and others were dead. I certainly deserve blame for not acknowledging sooner the receipt of that fine gift, but I was ashamed to write to you an empty handed letter, particularly as you had reminded me of the promised ferns, and multifarious duties delayed my attending to their business month after month.

---

[8] Definitely Baranetz, which I have not been able to identify.
[9] *Methonica* is an old generic name, = *Gloriosa* (LIL).

Better late than never, must be my excuse before you. I shall endeavor to make up by increased exertions for my past shortcomings.

By the end of next year I intend to make a trip to [illegible]¹⁰ Island, Bonabé or Pugaipet of several navigators, whither the missionary brig Morning Star makes a voyage every year from Honolulu. There is an American missionary stationed in that island who lately invited me to visit him and offered his assistance in collecting plants. I shall probably visit also some other islands of the Carolina group or Argolen and Eap [now Yap], probably also the low Coral Islands of the Kings Hill group and Ralik and Radach chains.

My principal object is to collect plants there and I should like to hear from you in what particular direction my research might become most valuable, also what works or voyages can be consulted with regard to the Vegetable productions of those islands. If you, or any of your friends, have any special direction to give to me, I shall take great pleasure to conform to them.

Let me remark here, that to the respective number of plants which are on the way for you, I have added a diagnostical name, in many instances much conjectural for I have no literary near on hand to determine them all correctly. My sources of reference were Beechey's Voyage and the US Explor. Expedition. The diagnosis are of course not considered of any value, they were intended only as collateral guarantee against future mistakes on my part in identifying plants you may have occasion to refer to. But you will greatly oblige me if you can as soon as possible, write to me, in return the true diagnosis of every individual number. Should you have any bulbs, tubers, plants or seeds to spare for my garden you would lay me under great obligations. In such case please to have the box sent to:

Manley Hopkins, Esq. The King of Hawaii's Chargé d'affairs and Consul General, Royal Exchange Hotel London. This gentleman will be directed by Mr. Wyllie to see the same forwarded hither by the most speedy & direct route via the West Indies steamer.

As before, tropical Orchidacea, Zingiberae, Liliacae, Amaryllidea, Aracea, Musaceae, Bromeliacea, Palms, etc. are my principal desiderata. But everything concerning this I leave to your discretion. Are ever seeds of the Mangosteen received in England? I have until now not been able to receive them from the places of their native growth. Can I receive seeds of this *Ravenalia* [sic] *Madagascar*?

Hoping, Sir, to receive soon a few lines in return, I remain with greatest respect and admiration your most humble servant
Wm. Hillebrand M.D., 1861

¹⁰ The word has been written over in the letter and is quite illegible; it must be an alternative name for modern Ponape, based on the context.

[Director's correspondence vol. 75, ff. 84]

Honolulu March 15, 1864
Sir W. J. Hooker
Dear Sir,

Your most esteemed letter of Sep. 23 last reached my hands on my return here from a prolonged visit to California, towards the close of the year. The sincere pleasure caused by reading the many expressions of kindness was however painfully alleged when I learnt the bad success which had attended my prior endeavor to oblige you. Having all along entertained a high opinion of the hardy nature and strong vitality of living flora, I certainly expected that, if not all, at last the greater part of them would reach you in good health. It may be that I watered them too freely before closing the cases. However, my motto is "*Nil desperandum.*" I shall try again soon in a different manner, packing strong rhizomes in powdered charcoal and closing them hermetically in tin boxes. I shall endeavor to persuade the first passenger who leaves direct for England via Panama to take charge of one, for experiments sake, and if it succeeds, the experiment may be repeated often. I am exceedingly desirous that your fine fern and palm houses should possess the beauties of our islands, if it were only for the sake of their country's reputation. In the meanwhile I am somewhat hopeful yet that Dr. Wood's case may have fared better. In fact, it was the expectation to hear of the "Hecate's" arrival in England which has caused me to put off the writing of this letter until now. Dr. W. carried with him a large number of mature seeds of our lowland <u>Loulu</u> palm of which I think some will germinate yet. I think it is a species of the new genus *Pritchardia* lately established by H. Wendland, as I saw in the Bonplandia.[11] I used to place it between *Livistona* and *Corypha*. I must state here, that several years ago, I gave to the late General Miller on two different occasions if I remember right, seeds of the lowland and mountain palm or <u>Loulu</u>, to be forwarded to you, but as they have not been acknowledged together with other specimen of plants given to him, I fear they never were forwarded. The lowland <u>Loulu</u> occur also at the Marquesas Islands as I gathered from the description of a person who saw it there, and from two seeds handed to me, and what is rather singular, it bears in the Marquesan language the name <u>Havane</u> which is given by our Islanders to its nuts which are eatable.

New ferns from our Islands I cannot send you at present because I have not found any, but as soon as I shall find time, I will make you up

---

[11] "Bonplandia" is a botanical journal published in France.

a collection of my grasses and mosses, amongst the former of which I trust, you will find some novelties. I will also make you up a collection of what I take to be new plants or at all events—rare, from my herbarium [collection], as soon as I shall have time to sort it.

When in California last summer, I have picked up a good many plants in the Sierra Nevada in which I made several extended excursions, having visited the Yosemite Valley and several groves of the Big Trees (Sequoia). In packing my bundles I was astonished, really to have found 18 species of ferns in that dry country, of which I shall transmit to you specimens as soon as the said bundles will be opened, which I have not have time yet to do, although, I dare say, you have received them all before those of the Sierra through Mr. Bridges. If you wish any other classes of plants from California I shall gladly communicate them to you, and what is not in my collection I shall be able to get from those of my friend H. Bolander or Prof. Brewer, both in San Francisco. The formers' specialties are mosses and grasses of which I have no doubt, he will be happy to send you what you may wish.

To your Botany in "Beechey's" I was indebted as my best guide through the mazes of the California Flora. Of the <u>pulu</u> Ferns I shall send you more perfect specimens, one of the new species (or varieties as may be) has the long leaf stalks beset with stiff, hairy bristles.

What you have mentioned about those new treasures, ready to be placed in my Wards cases have filled me with impatience, at the same time I do not know by which way to recommend you to send them. From Mrs. Staley, the Bishop's lady, whom I consulted about my trouble this afternoon, I learn that a vessel will be dispatched from Liverpool for this port some time after this letter will arrive in England and she has been kind enough to give me the address of their agent in London: John Shepherd and Co., Bishops Gate St, within No. 90, to whom she will write with regard to the cases, that he may advise you of the sailing of the vessel and take charge of the forwarding of the cases to Liverpool. The bark R. W. Wood has been here and sailed again, unfortunately while I was absent on the island of Maui, and from their owners I learn she will leave for Bremen again about October. If the Liverpool vessel should have a good deck, I think it would be preferable to send the cases by her. I should like greatly to receive a *Ravenalia* [sic] in them. Of your former plants a *Strelitzia* and 2 Bilbergias have flowered already. That I should like also to have the better kinds of *Cinchona*, I believe I wrote to you in my last letter. From an article in the Medico Chirurg. Quarterly I learn, that you keep a well stocked nursery of them at Kew. If it were possible, I should like to receive the plants by the way of Panama, but the transit over the isthmus is attended with so many difficulties, that I dare not to recommend it.

Your most liberal offer of part of your *Species Filicum*[12] has given me an extraordinary pleasure. I had more than once revolved in my mind the question of purchasing it, but the high price has hitherto deterred me. You may be assured that the gift will be most thankfully appreciated.

As you have not been able to find the Hawaiian Consul's name in the blue book, I will give you here his address: Manley Hopkins, Esq. HRM's Chargé d'Affaires and Consul General, 4 Royal Exchange Buildings, London. He is a very obliging gentleman and will, I have no doubt, be happy to forward anything you may entrust to his care. The same may be said of the Liverpool merchant who carries on the greatest part of the British Commerce with their Islands: R. C. Janion, Esq. the Albury, Old Hall St, Liverpool.

The next package of plants I shall be able to send off in 4 or 6 weeks. The rhizomes of ferns in a tin case may leave about the same time. Hoping that they will meet with better success, I remain dear Sir, most respectfully,
Your very humble and obd. [obedient] svt. [servant]
Wm. Hillebrand

---

[12] *Species Filicum* is a treatise on ferns written by W. J. Hooker.

[Director's correspondence vol. 75, ff. 86]

Honolulu Febr. 24, 1865
Sir Wm. J. Hooker
Dear Sir

      Your favor of Sept. 3 was received by me sometime in December. As in it you informed me that you had sent two cases of plants to Liverpool, to go with the "Meroia," I concluded to wait with the answer until arrival of said vessel. The same has come now, after a protracted voyage of 150 days, while a good trip ought not to take more than 120 or 130 days. My anxiety for the fate of the plants had been growing with every day of delayed hope during the last month, the more agreeable was my surprise to see the comparatively good condition in which the plants appeared on opening the boxes. Inside No. 1 there were 15 alive, 2 doubtful and 5 dead. In case 2, there were 10 alive, 9 dead, and 2 doubtful. I shall enclose a list indicating which plants arrived well, and which not. As it is, I feel highly gratified at the acquisition of so many fine plants for my garden and shall always remember you thankfully when admiring their growing beauty. In especial do I value the *Monstera deliciosa, Kniphofia uvaria,* those fine Bromeliads and the pretty *Meyenia,*[13] which although appearing quite dead at first sight, has already commenced to send out a fine healthy shoot. I greatly regret that some of the tropical water aroids of which you have repeatedly sent a whole set, of *Caladiums* for instance, ever have reached me alive. Unless there should be a chance to send them by the way of the isthmus, it would hardly be advisable to try them again. For those fine books, you have been so kind to send to me, I have to thank you most warmly. The *Species Filicum* are a real treasure to me; in the two last numbers I see that you have already noticed and described some of the ferns contained in the first lot I sent. That *Polypodium* which you have been kind enough to name after me, I had been long in doubt about whether it would constitute a new species, but I could not fully make up my mind to its being specifically distinct from *P. tamariscinum.* Let me here make one remark. If I have appended names to the numbers sent I have done so, in many instances, without being in the least certain whether the specimens so labelled corresponded with the species described by that name, and for this good reason <u>that I got a great</u>[14] many species. I had no description on hand but guessed at them simply from the position they occupied between others better known to me by the few books of reference then in my possession. Now, with the aid of the complete set of your *Species Filicum* that difficulty is removed. To Dr. J. Hooker, also please to express my

13 Word unclear—could be *Meyenia* (=*Thunbergia,* ACA), or *Meyenia* (CAC), or *Meyenia* (=*Cestrum,* SOL), or *Meyera* (=*Holosteum,* CRY), or *Meyera* (=*Enhydra,* AST).
14 These underlined words were written over in the letter and are unclear.

deep gratitude for the valuable publications which he has had the kindness to send. With the greatest satisfaction I have read that portion of his Introduction to the *Flora of Australia*, in which he speaks in so complimentary terms of the merits of my old friend Ferdinand Mueller of Melbourne.

For the last three weeks I have been busy to arrange my collection of plants so that I may be able to send you as complete a set of them as possible. Last night I reached #136 which includes the Syngenesiae,[15] Lobeliaceae, Goodenoviaceae, Ericaceae, Epacrid., Euphorb., Frangulac.,[16] Solanaceae, Leguminosae. It will be interesting to me, to find out by this enumeration the number of species contained in the flora of our Islands. My researches have only gone over the islands of Oahu, Maui, and Hawaii. From Kauai I have only a few stray specimens, but I intend to explore that island thoroughly. I shall send you specimens as good as I can afford them, of everything I have got; but what destruction the insects have made in them! Do not judge from the appearance of many, that I have collected carelessly, for I always made it a point to procure good specimen, in flower and fruit, and yet for lack of time the papers have remained untouched a whole year, a great deal is gone, the Convolvulaceae entirely. The Lobeliads have suffered badly, although I had touched the axillas and flowers with a solution of corrosive sublimate. I see now, that it is of no use unless the whole plant be dipped into it. Only I am somewhat afraid for my lungs which were badly affected with tubercular disease when I arrived here. Could you inform me what experience, if any, has been gained by the keepers of large herbaria on this point?

The collection destined for you I shall send off in about a month, by way of the isthmus. It is very probable that our sincerely beloved young widowed Queen Emma will visit England, in which case your commissioner Mr. Synge will accompany her, who has promised me to take care of anything I might have for you. If this project should fail, there is still another English gentleman here, Mr. Stephen Spencer, a government employee whom I shall ask to do me the favor as he will leave for England about the same time. I shall also try to make up for you a case of fern roots packed in charcoal powder in a tightly soldered tin case, as I have lately done for Mr. Van Houtte in Ghent, who gave me directions to that effect. In case our Queen should go, you would have a good opportunity to send me living plants by the isthmus as an English man of war would carry her direct from Panama back to these islands. Aroids and Musaceae and orchids would have a good chance of travelling

---

[15] "Syngenesiae" is a best guess, this is an alternate name for the Compositae.
[16] Frangulac. = Frangulaceae, now = Rhamnaceae.

safe. Do not young palm trees do well in glass cases even on long voyages? I have already 19 species of palms grown in my garden and they are my particular delight. From South America I have not got a single species yet. By the by, let me know if you have raised any plants from my <u>Loulu</u> seeds. I sent some to Mr. Van Houtte upon his request with direction to communicate you some, if they arrived in good order. To Dr. H. Wendland in Hanover I have sent complete specimens of that palm which will enable him to ascertain if it belongs to his new Feejeean genus *Pritchardia*. It seems to me that there is a remarkable difference in the many bracts enveloping the spadix of our <u>Loulu</u> palm.

In the matter of Ferns I shall be able to send you good specimens of some of the rarer kinds and one undoubtedly new *Polystichum* from the northern side of Mt. Haleakala, recently found there by Mr. Horace Mann, a young botanist from Boston, who has been collecting here for nearly a year for Prof. A. Gray. Upon my request he gave me two specimens, one for myself, and one for you, which therefore, when you describe it in the Supplement to the *Species filicum*, please to credit to him. I shall also add the ferns of my California collection of '63.

I shall have to hurry up matters as I shall start in a month on a long voyage which will absent me from here for a year or more. The case is this: The rapid development of the agricultural resources of our Islands (sugar, coffee, cotton and rice), together with the fatally progressing diminution of our native population has forced upon our Government the necessity of looking out for new sources of labor and population. Chinese immigrants were tried many years ago, but failed to give satisfaction. Still, to a small extent, they being the only immediately available source, they will have to be introduced first, to meet the existing wants. But in order to avoid the importations of the dregs of Chinese cities with which the regular Coolie Traders generally fill their vessels, the Government has concluded to send a special agent whose duty it will be, to go himself into the rural districts of Pokiew, and see that the local agents to be employed will only select a suitable class of people. From there the agent will have to go to Madras and Calcutta, to see how far the importation of the hill people from the Neilgheries and the foothills of the Himalaya is practicable and desirable and eventually to make there arrangements for that object. A collateral duty of the agent will be to investigate the subject of Oriental leprosy, which during the last 6 years has spread alarmingly among our people, and also in Ceylon, to gather information on the diseases affecting the coffee trees, a matter of the greatest importance to our coffee planters. This mission has been offered to me, of course I was only too glad to accept. A vessel has been chartered and I am to go as soon as my arrangements are completed. Now I shall have the best possible opportunity to bring here myself all those vegetable treasures which I have bothered my correspondents about [illegible] for so many years. You could do me a great favor if you would write a few lines to Dr. Thwaites in Ceylon and Dr. Anderson in Calcutta, recommending me and my object to these gentlemen. It will probably take 5 months before I shall reach Ceylon.

With regard to your wish to procure a section of the Big Tree, as they call the *Wellingtonia* in California, I have written to the proprietor of the Calaveras grove at whose hotel I spent two months in '63. If such a section as you desire, can be had for 5 guineas; I doubt somewhat as labor is very high there—$4 a day and the diameter of the only two trees which lay prostrate on the ground are, 10 feet from the base, 32 and 28 ft. Still, I feel sure it that, if the thing can be done, it will be done by the proprietor as he has shown himself very obliging towards me, and will take some extra pains, if he learns where the piece is to go to. In order that this business be not neglected during my absence, I have entrusted it to the care of my wife's father, Dr. Newcomb, in Oakland Calif., of whom you may have heard as a conchologist and friend of Mr. Hugh Cummings. I have requested him to disburse the money on my account and place the section on arrival in San Francisco under the care of the English consul. Dr. Newcomb will inform you in time of the result of the negotiation. A large piece of the bark you can get, probably without any expense. Mr. Brewer has left California for Harvard University and Dr. Bolander could be of little service to you in this matter as he has never been up to any of the groves in the Sierra Nevada.

Of the *Icones Plantarum* you have sent
Part viii 1841 ....Tab. CCCLI to Tab. CD
New Series Vol. II Part I (Tab. DI to Tab. DL) in duplo
New Series Vol. IV Part 2 (Tab. DCCLI to Tab. DCCC) in triplo
(probably by mistake)

Hoping that these lines will meet you in good health and [illegible] I remain, dear Sir, with most sincere veneration and unbounded respect
Your most obdt. svt. [obedient servant],
Wm. Hillebrand

I should like to see the new plants in my collection described as soon as possible.

[Director's correspondence vol. 75, ff. 85]

Honolulu April 1, [18]65
Sir W. J. Hooker
Dear Sir,

Your favor of orchids and other plants by Bishop Staley I have duly received in November last, and should have acknowledged before this, if I had not cherished the hope that perhaps a few lines from you would reach me. My warmest thanks for that fine collection. Six orchids, 3 Bromeliads and 1 *Strelitzia* arrived in good condition and are growing now.

Next week I shall send to you by the Bremen bark RW Wood and Capt. Geerken another collection of dried specimens of ferns, which, together with the one sent last year, will nearly complete the list of all the species described, to my knowledge, and add a few which I am deem to be new.

In fact, with exception of two *Ophioglossums*, and the *Trichomanes Drayton.* described by Brackenridge, I believe I have sent all that have been described in the American Expl. Expeditions section on ferns. These few missing species I expect to be able to send you before the end of another year. Allow me to call your attention to the species of *Cibotium* of which I send you four, the Akoléa, the Hapú, the Mauai and the I'i. The three latter produce Pulu and the Mauai and I'i are only found in the thick woods of Hilo district, on the flank of Mauna Kea. Specimens of the pulu pertaining to each you will find in the package. From the descriptions given in the work of the Am. Expl. Exped. I can only identify the Akolea or the *Cibot. Chamissonis* and the Hapu as the *Cibot. glaucum*. The description of *Cibot. menziesi* does not seem to me to apply to either the Mauai or I'i, but perhaps to the variety of the Akolea which grows on the island of Hawaii. The three pulu ferns are tall and stately trees; of the Hapu I have seen trunks measuring 3 ft. in diameter and 24 ft. in height, the crown of fronds adding 12 ft. more, makes the total height of the tree 36 ft.

The Mauai and I'i do not yield to the Hapu in size or stateliness, but exceed it in gracefulness. The Akolea never reaches this height. The rhizomes of all serve as food to the natives in times of scarcity of kalo. Other edible fern roots are those of the *Marattia alata,* or Pala, and of the *Nephrodium cyatheoides* or Kikawaeo. Besides these, the natives use as green vegetables the young fronds of the Palaiia *Deparia Prolifera* and of the *Diplazium Arnotti*. The glossy black stipes of the *Adiantum* and *Doryopteris pedata*, both called Iwa'iwa, are employed for making hats and bonnets.

The rhizone of the *Marattia*, which is rich in mucilage serves also for making a diet drink in diarrhea and bronchitis. Of the <u>Mauai</u> and <u>I'i</u> I shall endeavor to send you whole fronds, the stipe of one, I do not recollect which, is beset with black hair, those which I collected were unfortunately lost.

The R. W. Wood is a regular trader between Bremen and this port, making one voyage either way every year. She never had a longer passage from Bremen to Honolulu than 124 days. As Cpt. Geerken was so obliging as to offer to take two Wardian cases on board, which he promised to return filled with living plants, I considered the opportunity for sending you a lot of ferns for the new fern house in Kew, too good to be lost. I have therefore sent on board both cases filled with ferns and a few other plants, amongst which that beautiful climber *Freycinetia scandens*. Cpt. G. has orders only to forward them to you in case a good proportion of the plants arrive in good order. About the manner by which you will wish them to be sent to England please to communicate with L. Geerken, Bornstrasse No. 22, Bremen, the father of our captain. The Wardian cases please to return as soon as possible to Bremen, as they are to serve for the reception of other plants. If you would have put in them some plants of the families of orchids, Zingiberac., Bromeliads, Musaceae (*Ravenalia*), Aroids, Palms, Liliads, etc., You would certainly put me under great obligations, but after the many liberal favors received before, I hardly dare to ask. For many years past I have unsuccessfully endeavored to obtain for our Islands from the East Indies the Cinnamon, Clove, Nutmeg, the various peppers, the Mangosteen, Durian, and other fruit trees. If you could send young plants or fresh seeds of these, I do not know. The RW Wood will pass the Cape Horn on her return voyage in December or January so these plants would have the benefit of the Antarctic summer. I forgot to mention that between the ferns I have deposited many seeds of our <u>Loulu</u> palm, that species which grows near the sea which I had always taken to be *Livistona*, until I lately saw in the Bonplandia that Wendland refers it to his new genus *Pritchardia*. With it I put in seeds of our <u>Halapepe</u> tree, a tall *Cordyline*, or perhaps a new genus to be placed in its neighborhood. It has large, drooping racemes of bright yellow flowers. Its light wood served in former times for carving into idols. Probably some one will apply to you for a few young plants of these two trees in behalf of Mr. Linder of Brussels who had written to Mr. Wyllie to send him seeds. I trust that a sufficient number will germinate to satisfy his demands.

During the last week I had the pleasure to become acquainted with Dr. Wood, formerly of H.R.M.s ship Plumper, who arrived here in the Hecate. As he is anxious to bring you something from these islands, I have filled him a third Wardian case with ferns, which however will probably not reach you before 2 or 3 months, as the Hecate will proceed to England via Sidney and Batavia.

The Bermuda Arrowroot you sent before, but it was dead when it arrived, I should be happy to receive another plant of it. — As soon as I shall have leisure to arrange my collections I shall send to you specimens of all plants which I have not seen described or of such as are rare in our islands. To them I will add also my mosses and grasses; of the latter and Cyperacae I have about 56 species. Hoping to receive from you a few lines soon, I remain, dear Sir, with greatest respect and admiration
Yours most obediently
Wm. Hillebrand

P.S. Both the RW Wood and the Hecate are going to leave today Apr. 15. There will be no charge for freight on the Wardian cases.

see post script   *[Director's correspondence vol. 75, ff. 87]*

Honolulu April 12, 1865
Sir W. J. Hooker
Dear Sir,

My last letter left here about six weeks ago. In it I advised you
of the safe arrival of the two cases with plants and of my impending
visit to China and the East Indies. As I am just at the eve of starting for
these countries, I hasten to write you these lines and inform you, that
the collection of Hawaiian plants which I was preparing when I wrote
you last, is finished, packed and will be sent on board of H.M.'s sloop
of war Clio tomorrow. This vessel arrived two days ago, sent by orders of
the Admirality to carry our widowed Queen Emma and suite to Panama.
From/At Aspinwall,[17] the party to which is attached H.B.M.'s Consul
General and Commissioner Mr. P. Synge, will take the Southampton
steamer for England direct. Mr. Synge has kindly promised me to take
charge of the box and see that it be safely delivered to you. But I think
you will do well as soon as you learn of the arrival of the party in
England, to address our Hawaiian Consul General in London, whose
brother, Mr. Gordon Hopkins will be the Queen's Private Secretary, on
the subject.

There may be a small charge on it for transport across the
Isthmus; the West Indies steamer, I dare say, carry such articles free of
expenses. The collection comprises more than six hundred numbers, not
counting the ferns, mosses, lichens, etc. My algae, I am sorry to say, have
been lost, most unaccountably to me. If they should turn up yet, you shall
have them at later time. Of mosses and lichens I can only send you what I
collected during the last 18 months, as all that I had previous to that time
[illegible] given to Mr. H. Bolander of San Francisco whose specialty
mosses are. I have learnt since that he has communicated them for
inspection to Tuckerman and Lesquereux who I believe have described a
few new species from them.

You will find perfect specimens of the *Lobelia macrostachys* and
2 drawings of the same, one of a single branch, colored, by Mrs. Helen
Newcomb, my wife's mother, whose husband is well known to con-
chologists in England by his publications on Hawaiian landshells. I am
also happy to be able to send you specimens not only of both our
Hawaiian palms, the <u>Loulu</u> and <u>Havane</u>, but also of the one which grows

---

[17] "From" has been written over "At"; the Aspinwall seems clear but where is it?

on Bird Island, a large rock some 300 miles to the North West of this group. About six years ago our late King made an excursion to that island on the English frigate "Havana," whence he brought back a few young plants of that palm which he planted in the palace garden. One single plant survived and just has come in flower for the first time. I have secured a leaf of it and the first spadix for you. It does not seem to me to differ from our Loulu, or seaside palm, in any essential character, but the whole tree looks more robust and full and the leaves are larger. The fruit of course, I cannot send you now, but you shall have it later. The specimen of the <u>Havane</u>, or mountain palm, are the first which I have been able to obtain. I have seen a patch of the plant before, but in a place absolutely inaccessible. For these I had to send a native to the Northern side of the island, where I was informed a patch of these grew in a less difficult place. Unfortunately the man brought down neither flowers nor the bracts belonging to the spadix, although he received written instructions for the purpose.

This <u>Havane</u> palm has a trunk not higher than 4–5 ft., while the Loulu is from 15–20 ft. high, but its leaves are at least one third larger and covered with a white waxy substance on their under surface. The projection of the stalk in the frond is also different. As I wrote to you before, I have sent complete specimens of the <u>Loulu</u> palm to Mr. H. Wendland in Hanover on his request, and promised to send specimen of the <u>Havane</u> later. I leave it to you if you will let him have the temporary use of the specimens of <u>Havane</u> and Bird's Island <u>Loulu</u>, considering that Palms are his special delight. More complete specimen will follow. I expect also to receive specimens of this genus from the Marquesas with the return of the mission. schooner Morning Star, maybe before the Clio sails. In that case you shall have those also.

Amongst the other plants, I dare say, you will find a number of new ones, probably a few new genera. I cannot point out to you here the number which I believe to be so, but they are principally among the plants from the Kohala range on Hawaii, mostly from its Western terrain called <u>Kawaihae iuka</u>. You would greatly oblige me if you would look over the collection as soon as it arrives and single out what you recognize to be new. Might it not be well to publish a simple enumeration of them in a botanical journal, as B. Seemans Feejeean plants were in the Bonplandia? In proposing this I am led in part by a strong desire to see cleared up what is obscure to me yet in our flora, but besides I must own up to a somewhat

selfish motif. As I wrote to you before there is now here a young Boston
botanist, Mr. H. Mann, collecting for A. Gray. He is a very fine and indus-
trious young fellow whom I have taken pleasure to direct to the best of my
ability in his peregrinations. The consequence is that he has got a good
many new plants from places where I had been years before him and
where he went for the purpose of finding such plants according to information received by me. Now, although I am thankful to him for every new
plant he finds still I think, I might justly claim credit for what I found first.

I will state here that I have sent you the best specimens I had. If
many numbers are incomplete, the fault lies mostly with the destructive
insects. All my remaining specimens I have dipped in an alcoholic solution of corrosive sublimate, but yours have not been thus treated, because
I was not sure that it would be agreeable to you. Of others, as some of
the rarest Lobeliads which only grow in deep gulches where the sun finds
little access, I could only gather fragments of leaves. You will find a few
orchids which will relieve our flora from the stigma thrown on it by
some botanists, that it were destitute of them. That terrestrial orchid in
the woods of Hilo I have found with pink and yellow flowers, but I
could not make out any other characteristic distinction. Has ever a *Batis*
been collected here? If not, it is rather singular for it grows in salt marshes
quite near Honolulu. Of ferns I have not found but one new one since
my last lot was sent off, in fact I have not been able to make any, but
quite short excursions, but I have been enabled to send you some fine
specimens of our *minutice* [unclear word in gutter] in that line, as *Polyp.
minimum, Haaliliranum*, etc., Hymenophylleae, and *Trichomanes* as collected
on the highest mountain peak of our island, Konahuanui and Waipuhia.
Also a little *Ophioglossum* from the Wailuku Falls near Hilo. That new
species of *Polystichum* was found by Mr. H. Mann, who sends it with his
respects, on Haleakala.

A *Begonia*, I suppose which be something new from a Pacific
Island. The specimens were good, but have been almost ruined by the
insects, but I have the plant now growing in my garden. Another new
plant which has not flowered yet, I had brought to me by natives some
time ago and located in my garden. It has a tuberous root and five, large
fleshy pinnate leaves, is herbaceous. I take it to be an araliaceous plant. Its
native name is Makua.

Has Dr. Wood's case reached you? I have not heard either of him,
or of Hecate, since he left Honolulu.

Of my impending voyage to China and the East Indies, I entertain the most sanguine hopes. Our government, [illegible] being forced by necessity of increasing the population and labor force of our Islands, has appointed me a Commissioner for immigration from these countries. I have carte blanche to visit China, Singapore, Java, Ceylon, Madras and Calcutta, Mauritius and the Philippine Islands, and on my return I shall probably see Japan also. My first duty is to send as many good agricultural laborers with their families from China, Madras, or Calcutta as can be procured. They will have to engage themselves for a term of five years—to be bound to a plantation or farm at the rate of wages ruling in this country. As plantation labor is very light here and good laws give effective protection to the laborer, there is little doubt but that most of the immigrants will be a permanent acquisition.

My second duty will be to investigate and report on the measures resorted to in those countries against the Oriental leprosy, which disease, although of not more than 12 years standing here, is causing great alarm to this people.

My third duty is to introduce useful plants and animals from those countries and for this purpose both our Agricultural Society and Government have placed funds at my disposal with considerable liberality. In furthering this objective which [illegible] lies nearest to my heart, you could lend me very effective assistance, if, in writing to your botanical and other friends in those countries, you would just mention my name in a few short lines. Dr. Thwaites and the *Cinchona* trees in the Peredeniya Gardens are most prominent in my view. Now I expect to get the spice trees, the mangosteen, the teak, [illegible] from their own native countries. It is a realization of a dream which I have long carried with me. You may be sure that I shall pick up every fern that comes in my way for on the principal that a good thing need only be tasted to grow a liking to it, so the study of ferns, to which I have been introduced by you, has exerted its attraction over me. – Besides the above duties, I shall have to report on the coffee disease in Ceylon and on the state of agriculture in these countries in general.

Our package in the box contains the ferns collected by me in summer of 1863, in California, mostly in the Sierra Nevada between Calaveras and Fresno County. I am sorry not to have had the time to have made you up a suite of all the other plants collected there, for, although you have undoubtedly received many collections from that [illegible] I have little doubt, that I can give you a good many new plants from the Sierra, particularly it's Alpine portion. After my return I shall try to make you up a suite.

I am in hourly expectation of a China bound vessel and may therefore not have time to make you up any living plants, but if possible, I will see that the Clio may take a lot of fern roots packed in powdered charcoal. The Queen will return by the way of Panama and in all probability Bishop Staley will have joined her in England, to return with her. That would be a capital opportunity to get living plants here in good condition. The Bishop will do me the favor to call on you and take charge of anything you may have for me. Aroids and orchids would have a good chance to travel safely, not to forget the ornamental Musaceae. Can you send seeds of the *Victoria Regina* or even young plants? They could be taken care of during the whole voyage. But I must conclude my long letter.

Should you be kindly disposed to write me a few lines in answer to this letter, please to send them to the care of Dr. Thwaites in Ceylon, as I expect to be in that island about five months hence.

Hoping that heaven may preserve you in good health and grant you many years of happiness to yourself and usefulness to science. I am, dear Sir, with the sincerest expressions of admiration and devotion
Your most obdt. [obedient] svt. [servant]
Wm. Hillebrand

I must again call to your mind, that the diagnoses which I have appended to many plants have very little weight with me as I have not had time to examine most plants otherwise but very superficially. They are intended chiefly to be an additional means of identifying the plants with those in my herbarium. The native names, whenever they were known to me, have been written in the left upper corner of the label.
Dare I ask you for your photograph?

[A small piece of paper, evidently enclosed in the finished letter, is affixed to the first page. It reads:]
I have just become enabled to lay in the box a leaf and flowering spadix of the palm from Bird's Island.[18]

---

[18] The specimen survives at Kew, stored in the oversized material in the Palm section. It is identified as *Pritchardia hillebrandii*.

[Director's correspondence vol. 178, ff. 234]

Honolulu, March 12, [18]67[19]

Dear Sir,[20]

My good friends Mr. and Mrs. G. Rhodes are leaving for Europe tomorrow for a flying visit from which they will return by the end of this year. Allow me to recommend them to your particular favor so that they may be enabled to see all the wonderful plants of the Kew Gardens and the wealth of its Museum. As I have never been there yet myself, I hope to derive considerable pleasure from the account which they will give me.

By the last mail I had the great satisfaction of receiving your cases of February 1 with the enclosure of Mr. LeNormand. I shall be very glad to satisfy that gentleman's wishes as soon as possible and shall write to him to that effect.

The introductory letters of your revered father, whose memory will ever be blessed by all who had any relations with him, have been of the greatest service to me during my late visit to China, Java and Calcutta. Sickness prevented me from going to Ceylon and seeing Dr. Thwaites, but before leaving Hong Kong, I had a very friendly letter from him accompanied by a Wardian case with fine plants, a package of seeds and specimens of ferns. Altogether I have brought to these Islands from those countries 34 Wardian cases full of plants and several thousand packages of seeds.

As soon as my various duties will allow me, I shall make excursions to procure you fresh seeds of Lobeliaceae and other plants. Those of the *Argyroxiphium* do not ripen before August. Our geraniums also will become very ornamental greenhouse plants.

You are kind enough to ask what you can send me from Kew. As Mr. Rhodes will return direct from England to Honolulu, it would be a capital opportunity to send something by him. Tubers or bulbs of any kind—Gesneriads, Amaryllis, Lilliaceae, such orchids as will stand dry packing, particularly American, Bromeliacea, Musaceae, all this will be welcome. So also will be seeds of palms and spores of arborescent ferns. (I have raised quite a number of Indian ferns from spores) and a small collection of choice annuals.

With regard to Bromeliads I will remark, that I am already in possession of *Aechmea fulgens*, of *Bilbergia speciosa, Wetherelii, amoena, zocata* and *pyramidalis* and of *Vriesia* spec. These species need therefore not to be

---

[19] The month is problematic because "May" and "March" have been written atop one another and it is impossible to know which is meant. I am using March based on para. 2, where Feb. 1 is cited.

[20] End of letter: "Dr. Jos. Hooker & etc."

sent. Of Musaceae I have growing fine plants, of *Strelitzia regina* and *angusta* and *Musa coccinea.*

I have made a considerable collection of specimens of plants in China, (Hong Kong, Macao, Canton) and Java; but as you have had so many collectors in those countries, I can hardly expect to be in a position to offer you anything new. It is hardly necessary for me to say that of new or interesting plants which I may in future find on these islands you will always receive the first specimens.

Hoping to be from time to time favored with a few lines from your hand, I have the honor to remain, dear Sir,

Your most obdt. [obedient] and humble svt. [servant]

Wm. Hillebrand

[Director's correspondence vol. 178, ff. 235]

Honolulu Sept. 23, [18]67

My dear Sir,[21]

   With the present I send you a parcel containing 28 packages of seeds as a first installment. They are quite fresh, nearly all collected within the last 3 or 4 weeks, and will reach you, I trust, in good condition. I regret not to have been able this time, to send you any Lobeliaceae and such Syngenesious plants as are characteristic of our island flora, but expect to come into possession of some soon. The Argyroxiphioms have ripe seed just now, but unfortunately they are preyed upon by a small insect which seldom leaves any whole ones on the plant, those which I sent to your father some 8 years ago cost me a great deal of trouble to obtain. I have, however, the promise of a person who resides some distance up on Haleakala, that I shall have some soon.

   Please to communicate a few seeds of the "<u>Hoolei</u>" to Prof. Oliver, for this is the species of *Ochrosia* No. 318 which was marked by him as "sp.n. or Sandw. var." As seeds of the *O. Sandw.* are also in this collection, it will be evident, I daresay, that it is a very distinct species; the *O. Sandw.* is a small tree, whose native name is "<u>Hao</u>."

   The perusal of your discourse on Insular Flora has been very instructive to me and I could wish that you would follow up the [unclear[22]] of the laws; laid down therein, with regard to the island groups of the Pacific. All the ideas brought forward by you meet with abundant proofs to substantiate them, in our flora. If I had more comprehensive material on hand covering those island groups next to us, the Marquesas, Society, Carolines, and Ladrones[?], I might take courage to take up this subject, but as it is, I will make up, for my own satisfaction a tabular synopsis of the places falling under each of the categories presented by you, and, in especial, point out those species of our autochthonous plants which are evidently verging towards extinction.

   Will you have the kindness to point out to me in which papers or journals Marquesan plants have been described? On Tahiti I have Beechey, Guillemin's, *Zephyritis Tahiti*[23] and Gray's *Botany "Expl. Exped."* I also possess Miquel's *Flora Ind. Batava*, which is quite useful for plants common to Polynesia and Malaya, and Bentham's *Flora Hong Kong*. Has B. Seemans *Flora of the Feejee Islands* appeared, or his projected *Enumeratio plant. Polynes.*?

   I have had very little time to botanize this summer; still I have made several additions to my herbarium, which I shall communicate to

21 End of letter: "Sir Joseph D. Hooker & etc etc"
22 Looks like "coolation," could be "correlation," or "collation."
23 The correct title of this obscure work is *Zephyritis tahitensis.*

you by the first vessel bound to England or Germany. Amongst them are good many Algae for Mr. Le Normand. At the same time I shall have some stone implements and minerals to add.

I was really glad to receive in your last letter the list of my California ferns, from the hand of your late father, but I never have had the determination of the Hawaiian ferns sent in 1862 and 63 [or 65?].

There is a vessel expected soon from Liverpool, which, I hope, will bring the box with bulbs and seeds spoken of in your former letter. Any favors of that kind will always be in the highest degree appreciated by me, particularly orchids. Might I also ask the favor of you, to send occasionally a few *Cinchona* seeds of the different species, which, I dare say, are now yearly send to Kew from India? I had seeds from Ceylon and Java, but they having been detained too long on the way, 5–6 months, they had lost their vitality. By way of Kew, if send in a letter, the transmission need not take more than 3-1/2 months, at most. Could you also put me in communication with any of the Bot. Gardens in the W. Indies for exchange of seeds—Jamaica or Trinidad?

I have not added any remarks to the seeds sent. A few belong to the coast vegetation, most of the others belong to the middle forest zone 1000–3000 ft. elevation. Only the *Edwardsia, Polycoelium*,[24] and *Cyathodes* rise above it. The *Erythrina, Edwardsia* and perhaps also the Dracaena aurea (by the bye, the only indigenous–Dry of which I have before sent seeds to Kew) alone have a season of rest. The *Chenopodium Sandw.* grows at 6000 ft. elevation in Hawaii to a tree of about 20 ft. in height. Its habitat, however, ranges from 1500–7000 ft. The *Capparis Sandw.* is a very hand-some plant, delighting in the driest and most rocky condition. It is, by the by, probably the same as the species of the Molucca Islands, which I saw in Buitenzorg. *Heliotropium anomalun* is well worth cultivating.

Hoping to be soon favored again with a few lines from you, I remain, dear Sir, most respectfully
your very obdt. [obedient] svt. [servant] Wm. Hillebrand

---

[24] *Polycoelium* is a synonymous name, = *Myoporum sandwicenis* A. Gray.

[Director's correspondence vol. 178, ff. 237]

Honolulu Febr. 23, 1868
Dear Sir,[25]

Your most acceptable lines of Nov. 24 [18]67 arrived here by the last mail. The envelope contained besides a paper with *Cinchona succirubra* seeds and a list of Sandw. Isl. ferns—for which you have my warmest thanks. The latter will be a great help in the determination of my specimens.

Of your kind permission to [illegible words] the use of your name in writing to the Curators of the Bot. Gardens in Jamaica and Trinidad, I have already availed myself and I feel confident that it will procure me the good will of those Gentlemen.

I am sorry to learn that part of my first parcel of seeds have been destroyed by a nasty weevil, but hope that the following packages which have left since—three if I remember right—have met with a better fate. With the present I send a few more seeds, the most important of which is the second species of *Pritchardia,* that one which grows on rocky cliffs near the sea and on high precipices on Oahu and Molokai. Of the first species you must have trees growing in Kew from seeds sent by me several years ago. This second one is smaller than that and is distinguished by the larger fruit which is round, not oval, and by the glaucous appearance of the underside of the frond, destitute of the woolly tomentum which covers the ribs and base of the frond in the former species. The nuts of both are eaten by the natives, although they are rather insipid, and the fronds are in great request for making hats and fans. A few seeds of this second species were in one of the former packages, but the present ones are fresher and perfectly ripened.

With regards to the determinations of the seeds sent I must claim some indulgence. Most of them come to me from a few friends on other islands who sent the seeds with the native names, if they can obtain such, but more frequently without any names at all. My determination must therefore, be in many cases, inaccurate, particularly with seeds of Compositae and Rubiaceae.

The list of S. Isl. Ferns sent in your last enclosure does not contain all the ferns sent by me; so there is only one *Trichomanes* mentioned viz. *T. parvulum.* Many of our most common ferns are omitted too, as *Gleichenia dichotoma,* Davallia tenuifolia, Microlepia hirta, and others. But it may be that they are not mentioned because they occur in many other countries, besides our islands. Mr. Oliver, in his second letter, made

---

[25] Bottom of first page of letter: "Dr. J. D. Hooker."

inquiry about an *Ophioglossum* found by Brackenridge on the Wailuku sandhills Maui. I have searched in that locality myself and made inquiries of people living there about such a plant, but with negative results. But I have found a very small *Ophioglossum* amidst the grass near the Wailuku Falls near Hilo, Hawaii, which I enclosed carefully wrapped in separate paper in a letter to your late father, and which must still rest amongst his collections. I have only one specimen left which stands at your disposal, if the other one should be lost.

I feel confident that Brackenridge's fern was found in the same locality, for the "sandhills of Wailuku" Maui, are dry and exposed to the sea, where no *Ophioglossum* can grow.

At *Asplen. Arnotti* I find marked in pencil the question: Is the caudex erect or decumbent? It is erect, arborescent from 1–3 ft. high. Which is Seeman's work in course of publication, the flora of the Feejees or the *Enumeration of Polynesian plants* and what will be the price of the work when finished?

I have in the course of last summer collected several plants not sent before, among which a very marked new species of *Cyrtandra*, which I shall send by the first opportunity.

The box with seeds sent by you to the Haw. Consul at Liverpool, Mr. R. C. Janion, has not arrived yet, and, unless you requested him to send it on per steamer in a "sample box", I fear it will go by sailing ship round Cape Horn, in which case there will be great loss. Any future missives[26] please to direct him to send in the manner indicated.

A list of species and habitats extracted from Seeman's new work will be very welcome to me. Hoping that you will excuse the desultory[27] character of this letter, I remain, dear Sir, yours most faithfully
Wm. Hillebrand

---

[26] This sentence is written very small, and fitted into a gap at end of a line; the word could be "missions" or "missives," as I have taken it.
[27] Also unclear as part of the word is written into the gutter; "desultory" fits the context.

[Director's correspondence vol. 178, ff. 241, 242 on P.S.]

Honolulu, July 20, 1868
Sir Joseph D. Hooker
My dear Sir,

I regret that I cannot find your last letter at the moment, so that I might be able to answer every point touched upon therein. However, I shall try my best to do so from memory. The seeds of the *Cinchona succirubra* and Latakia tobacco have arrived in excellent condition, and of both a great number of plants have been raised as well by myself as by the Makee's plantation which is situated on the Southern slope of Mt. Haleakala at an elevation of 2400 ft. the forest region thereto belonging extending up to 7000 ft. I hope and trust that the Cinchona will do well in the rich balsaltic scoria soil of that region. Since then I have received another package of *succirubra* from Dr. Thwaites, and by the last mail of *calisaya* from Dr. Teijsman in Java. The *officinalis* and *condaminea* are two other good species of which I remain in want yet.

You ask my opinion about the merits of *Kadua* as a genus. As I am acquainted with only a few of its many congeners amongst Hedyotideee, I do not presume to hazard an opinion on that point but I [illegible] send you with the present tolerably good seeds of such of my species as have any, 8–9. I hope they will enable you to arrive at a satisfactory opinion on that point. I send also with this seeds of the *Santalum paniculatum* which only grows at elevation exceeding 6000 ft. and of our 3 finest *Hibiscus*, the most interesting of which, our Kokio, seems not to have been described as yet, as I learn from a letter of Mr. Mann. I had hitherto taken it to be the *H. Arnottii* A. Gr. while his real *H. Arnotti* is the *H. Boryanus* of my herbarium. I send it as *H. Kokio*. It stands near the *H. rosa-sinensis*. I had expected to send you *Argyroxiphium* seeds this time, as my son, a boy of 14 years who has been spending his vacation in Maui, made the ascent of the mountain for this very purpose but he reports "not ripe yet." In September I shall probably go over myself, and hope to meet with better success.

Persian tobacco I have not received from you yet.

That precious package of Mauritius palms has not arrived yet, and by the last mail Mr. Janion writes that he has a parcel from you, undoubtedly the one in question, which he intends to send via Cape Horn so as to arrive here in October, just a year from the time it left Mauritius. Is not that provoking? Do not send anything again by Mr. Janion.

I have made arrangements with the principal of the firm Ed Hofschlager—a Bremen House—in this place to allow me to have any packages from you send through their Manchester friends Kessler & Co. They receive from them by <u>every</u> steamer goods as "slow freight" via Panama. The charges are very moderate and the voyage generally takes a little over two months. Mr. Hofschlager will probably send you a note with regard to the matter, or, if you would drop a line to Messrs. Kessler & Co., Manchester, they will give you the necessary information at once. Whatever palm seeds you can send me from Kew will be most welcome, as in fact any seeds likely to prosper here as also bulbs and in particular orchids.

By the barque R. W. Wood which leaves in 3 days for Bremen, I shall send a collection of specimens from my herbarium for Mr. R. Lenormand.

[end page missing]

[Director's correspondence vol. 178, ff. 243]

Honolulu Febr. 4, 1869

My dear Sir,

The Liverpool vessel with the Wardian case of living plants and a box containing bulbs and dry plants arrived here about the end of November. Of the fine collection in the Wardian case only the following were alive, and of these, those marked with an X have been in my garden for some time:

> X *Andropogon ciliatum*
> *Guatteria caffra*
> *Doryanthes excelsa*
> *Philodendron erubescens*
> X *Euphorbia splendens*
> *Clivia nobilis*
> *Acanthus montanus*

Of the Bromeliads the *Bromelia sceptrum* was the only one which showed signs of life and has since come out well, but the bulbs and tubers arrived in very good condition, only two or three of the smaller species having perished. Of the seeds also quite a number have come up well, amongst which I most appreciate the *Guaiacum officinale*, which always had failed me before, when I received it. The *Leucadendron argenteum* also has come up. While therefore I have greatly lamented the loss of so many fine treasures still I consider myself very much enriched by what has survived the perils of the long voyage, and can hardly express to you what delight you have caused me by your generous gift. Do the *Medinillas*[28] seed in Kew, if so, you would do me a great favor by enclosing some seeds in one of your letters, as also of species of *Nepenthes*.

If there has been such a long interval between this letter and my last one, the reason is, that I have not had any time either to make botanical excursions or to work in my herbarium. Besides my private practice, I have charge of the Queen's Hospital and of the insane asylum, and am connected with a few branches of our Government, as Board of Health and B. of Immigration, which latter, although honorary officer, have of late devolved a great amount of work on me. In fact, whatever time I have devoted to Botanical pursuits hitherto, have been an occasional day or a few weeks vacation snatched from my other duties. Since my excursion to the field of the Hawaiian earthquakes in last April, I have not been able to absent myself more than a

---

[28] The word is unclear; Medinilla is a genus with several ornamental shrubs and fits the context.

couple of hours from Honolulu and the only plants collected are Alga for Mr. Lenormand.

There are some plants in my herbarium which you have not had from me yet, they shall come as soon as possible. I see that B. Seeman has made a new Araliaceous genus *Dipanax*. This is perhaps the Araliaceous tree from the Kohala range in Hawaii, of which I sent specimens more than a year ago. I found flowering and fruiting specimen of perhaps another species (Gray's *Gastonia Oahuensis*) on the mountain back of Honolulu. I have also a new *Hibiscus* tall shrub of the —— section.[29]

I have collected some stone implements which I shall send you by first ship opportunity.

As a curiosum I must tell you, that in the collection of Palm seeds from Mauritius which came in the same vessel with your plants, consequently after a voyage of 13 months, there were quite a number of seeds—apparently species of *Areca* ([illegible] were all rotten) in a healthy state of germination. They were packed in charcoal, enclosed in a hermetically soldered tin case.

With this I send some seeds of *Santalum ellipticum* from Hawaii. They have grown on the high plateau 6000 ft. above the sea and will be suited to the temperate green house.

Hoping that these lines will reach you in good health I remain, dear Sir, most respectfully
Your obdt. [obedient] svt. [servant]
Wm. Hillebrand

---

[29] Hillebrand left a blank space, evidently intending to fill in the name of the section, but forgot.

[Director's correspondence vol. 178, ff. 244, 245]

Honolulu Octob. 17, 1869
Sir Joseph D. Hooker
My dear Sir,

The last mail brought me the long expected *Synopsis filicum*. Many thanks for the fine present; it just came in time to assist me most materially in the already commenced arrangement and labeling of my collection. I will also acknowledge here, if I have not done it before, the receipt of two packages of Conifers and one of *Cinchona officinalis*, which have arrived in the course of last summer. The Cinchonas promise to do very well. About 800 *succirubras* and *calisayas* have been set out already and about 1000 more await transplanting from boxes. As I wrote you before I have sent all the seeds to the Makee plantation on the southern slope of Mt. Haleakala, East Maui, where they are being set out in various enclosures, ranging from 2200 to 4000 ft. The soil there is exceedingly rich, being chiefly formed by the decomposition of the black sand (Basaltic and rapilli). Our common forest trees, which elsewhere do not grow to more than 25 ft. attain heights there of 60–80 ft. A very intelligent German gardener, H. Holstein,[30] has charge of them. To the same place I have also sent the conifer seeds.

I am sorry to hear that the Deodar seeds have all failed. Can you send them again? And do you ever receive seeds of *Podocarpus cupressina* and of *Altingia excelsa*, the rasamala tree of Java? But before all I would request you to continue to send the different species of *Cinchona*.

I had intended this summer to make long excursions over the Island of Kauai, but unfortunately a heavy pressure of professional business prevented me. Still I managed to steal away for a fortnight which I spent in the Kaala[31] range on this island. Three new species amongst which a terebinthaceous tree, and several of our rarest plants, as the *Alsinedendron trinerve*, have been the reward of much hard climbing. I shall send you of all by the first party that shall leave for Europe and be willing to carry the bundles. Botanizing on our islands is not without considerable danger. Only imagine my being obliged to descend a steep talon of at least 70°, which had to be done chiefly by swinging from the roots of one tree to the branches of the next one below, and that from a height of 2000 ft. above the deep gorge below.

By the last mail I did sent you a parcel of seeds which I gathered on those mountains. Amongst them is a *Viola* which surprised me by size

---

[30] Hermann Holstein.
[31] Ka'ala Range is an old name for the Wai'anae Mt. Range on W. O'ahu.

and beauty of its snow white waxy flowers. It is probably only a variety of *V. chamissionis* which I found in its ordinary state lower down in the forest, but this variety, growing on one of those razor back ridges, the showy flowers stretching on their long peduncles far above the surrounding low shrubbery and luxuriating in the full sunshine of an azure blue sky, exceeds the former so much by the size and beauty of its flowers (some were almost 1-1/2 inches in diameter) that I at first felt quite sure, I had discovered a new species. It will be well worth cultivating; grows at an elevation of 2000 ft. and more. On Mt. Kaala (4000 ft) I picked *Polypod[ium] rugulosum*, which, as coming from our islands, was quite a novelty to me, but now, to my surprise I see that the *Synopsis* gives the Sandwich Isld. also as its habitat. On whose authority has that been? Can the plant have been in my collection, for I was on the mountain before in 1861.

May I be allowed to ask you to communicate to me some duplicate specimen of ferns for my herbarium? I shall always be ready to send to you of our ferns in exchange which, although they may be represented already in the Kew Herbarium, still I think, will be useful for the purpose of exchange. My collection has, besides S. Isl. ferns, most of the Californian, many from North America and Europe, most Hong Kong ferns, a great many from Java and Ceylon (the latter through the kindness of Dr. Thwaites). From tropical America, Africa and Australia I have hardly any. Of my Java ferns I shall send you duplicates.

Hoping I shall have the pleasure, before long, to receive a few lines from you, I remain, dear Sir, most respectfully,
Yours truly, Wm. Hillebrand

[Director's correspondence vol. 178, ff. 238, 239]

Honolulu, Oct. 31

My dear Sir,

Your most appreciated lines of July 31 arrived at my hands two weeks ago. I had already learned from Mr. Rhodes how much kindness he and Mrs. R. had received from you on their visit to Kew, for which I do indeed feel exceedingly obliged to you. The biographical sketch of your late father, I am sorry to say, has not reached me; I need not express to you how much pleasure it will afford me to read anything bearing on the memory of that honored man.

With this I send you again a few seeds as they have just come to hand from East Maui, of *Pittosporum confertiflorum* A. Gr. and of our *Vaccinium reticulatum*, the fruit of which is quite palatable and which, as it grows at an elevation of 4–7000 ft. will probably stand the climate of the SW coast of England or Ireland. I also add seeds of the *Antigonon leptopus* from the Mexican coast which is a great favorite in our garden and, when fully in flower with its graceful festoons of pink and crimson spikes, may well compare for beauty with the *Bougainvillea*. I have another species in my garden with white flowers of which I shall be able to send you seeds in about a month.

My last letter to you left here 6 weeks ago and with it went a parcel with 28 packages of seeds. Two weeks ago I sent another parcel containing 23 packages, without a letter, which, I hope, have come to your hands before this. I had at first some hesitation about sending parcels of that size, but Mr. Wodehouse H.R.M.s Commissioner was kind enough to assure me, that he would always be ready to forward such and heavier ones. They went by the address indicated in your letters. The last collection came from Mt. Haleakala, and I had some difficulty in identifying a few of the seeds. I cannot vouch for the correctness of three of the names given to the seeds.

The seeds marked *Caesalpinia* are said to come from a small tree with bipinnate leaves, which is unknown to me. It might possibly be H. Mann's *Caesalpinia kauaiensis*. The native name of that is 'Uki' while that given for these seeds is 'Kea'.

Seeds of *Argyroxiphium* have not arrived yet. I had written to two parties before, and have now applied to a third one, requesting him to send a native expressively for this purpose up the mountain. As it takes a whole days hard travelling to obtain them, there is some difficulty in the way, but I hope to see them arrive before the departure of the next mail.

About 3 weeks ago the US steamer <u>Lackawana</u> left this port to survey a small corral island, called Middle Brook Isl., on 28.30' N.L. about 163
W. Long., some 500 miles distant from our group, which it was thought,
might afford a suitable coaling station for the California-China steamer line.
An officer of that vessel was kind enough to collect at my request specimens
of the plants growing on that small piece of rock about half a mile in diameter
and 40 ft. above the level of the ocean. Imperfect as these specimens were, I
could identify:

> *Ipomoea maritima*
> *Capparis Sandwicensis*
> *Tribulus cistoides*
> *Boerhavia diffusa*
> *Scaevola (sericea?)*
> *Lepidium Oahuense*

Besides these there were leaves apparently of a Borraginaceous plant, a
Solanum and of a Grass.

I believe I communicated to you in my last letter the request, to favor
me occasionally with a small paper of *Cinchona* seeds of the various species, as
they may come to your hand from India.

With regard to a moderate sized package or one with seed, tubers or
bulbs, it would reach me probably in 70 days, if you would be good enough
to transmit it to the Hawaiian Consul in Liverpool Mr. R. Janion, with the
request to send it along with a "Samples" for his house in Honolulu, as "slow
steamer freight." The expense of goods sent this way is only 40 cts. a pound,
which I could pay here on arrival. Mr. Green, Janion's partner in this place, has
assured me that he would write Mr. J. with regard to this matter.

Seeds of palms; tubers and bulbs of Geseriads, Lilys, Amaryllids, before
all orchids, could well travel that way.

I lately had the chagrin to lose my only *Sabal umbraculifera*, raised from
seed received by your late father about 6 years ago, by the ravages of our sugar
cane borer, the larva of a kind of weevil, and, since, that pest has destroyed several *Pritchardias* and began to attack other palms. I cut them out when their
presence can be discovered outside. Is there any means to keep off their inva-
sion?[32] Of course I have removed every stalk of sugar cane from the garden.

Please, do remember me kindly to Prof. Oliver and believe me, dear
Sir, to be most devotedly your most obdt. [obedient] svt. [servant]
Wm. Hillebrand

---

[32] Word is unclear – it could easily be "incursion".

[Director's correspondence vol. 178, ff. 246]

Honolulu, Febr. 8, 1870

Dear Sir,[33]

   I hasten to send you at the last hour before the closing of the mail a few good seeds of one of our rarest and most showy plants—the Lobelia gaudichandii which I collected 3 days ago near the top of Konahuanui, the highest peak of this island—4000 ft.

   If you will give me the address of a reliable correspondent of yours in New York I should like to make the experiment of sending you rhizomes of ferns, packed in tin cases filled with charcoal. The expenses per Pacific Railroad for a small case cannot be very high. The plants would reach you in about a month.

Most respectfully, in haste

Yours very truly

Wm. Hillebrand

---

[33] End of letter: "Dr. J. D. Hooker."

Honolulu, March 18, 1870
Sir Joseph D. Hooker
Dear Sir,

Your favor of January 1, including 3 packages of Cinchona and 2 of Tobacco seeds arrived by the mail steamers a few days ago, for which please do receive my warmest thanks. I am happy this time to be enabled to send you the long expected seeds of Argyrosiphion. I owe them to the kindness of Dr. Waivra, who has spent some time here in botanizing, he being attached as chief surgeon to the Austrian frigate <u>Donau</u>. A heavy typhoon disabled the vessel some days after she left Yokohama to such an extent that she had to put in here to undergo extensive repairs.

The Argyrosiphion grows on the rim and at the bottom of the extinct crater of Mt. Haleakala on Maui at an altitude of from 8–10,000 ft., between loose lava rocks. [Line illegible.] Near the freezing point in some [illegible] the mountain is snow-capped, but the noonday heat, owing to the reflection of the sun rays from the high rocks is the receiver of which the plant has its favorite habitat, is very great, not much below 84–86 degree. It rains a great deal on the mountain, but as the lava is very porous and so marshes crust[?] anywhere on it, I should think that the plant requires to be placed in well drained pots. A few other seeds go along. As soon as I have finished the arrangement of the plants collected during the last year, I shall transmit to you a parcel of specimens, amongst which are several new species, and it may be one new genus.

Is there any reasonable chance for orchids, packed dry in saw dust or coal to reach me safely, if send by the pacific Railroad? I should gladly pay the expenses for freight from New York and if they were directed to the care of HRH's Consul in San Francisco, Mr. Booker, they would be faithfully forwarded. Could the Musa Eirete[?] travel in the same way? Other [illegible] will stand transmission, packed dry, almost better than in Wardian cases. I have raised a number of Ravenalia plants from your seeds.

Hoping to hear from you soon, I have the honor, to remain dear Sir, with greatest respect,
Yours very faithfully. Wm H.

[Director's correspondence vol. 178, ff. 248]

Lahaina, Aug. 19, 1870

My dear Sir,[34]

      Having just returned from a trip up the high mountain which constitutes the Western half of the island of Maui, and learning that a schooner is going to leave for Honolulu in an hour, to connect with the mail steamer for San Francisco, I hasten to dispatch the enclosed package of seeds of *Lobelia Gaudich.*, one of the most showy plants of our Archipelago. A slender trunk of about 3 ft.[35] supports a crown of lanceolate leaves, from the center of which rises a raceme of magnificent cream-colored flowers, often subtended by several smaller ones which take their origin lower down. I have also gathered fine specimens in flower of the *Wilkesia*, but no fruit. By the last mail you must have received good seeds of the *Hillebrandia Sandw.* which I gathered in the isle of Molokai and forwarded w/o delay. It is the most showy *Begonia*, when in flower, with which I am acquainted. In a month I hope also to have secured good seeds of the *Brighamia insignis* which likewise grows in Molokai, but was not in seed when I saw it. I have now been absent from Honolulu over two months on a botanizing tour which comprises the islands of Molokai, Lanai and West Maui, which has resulted in quite a number of new species and at least two genera new to our group, one a sapotaceous tree and the other Myrsinaceous shrub. Besides these I have what Seeman probably has described as *Gossypium drynarioides,* in good flower and fruit, the latter a woody capsule of 5 cells, each cell containing only one lightly tomentose seed. I conclude from the latter circumstance, that it ought to constitute a new genus It is a tree of 15–20 ft. height. Another novelty I gathered last year, a tree, probably of the Terebinthaceae of which my former collections contained a few [illegible words written over] specimens, which were referred to *Ochrosia*. Three new *Cyaneas;* 2 new *Violas;* are amongst the results of my present expedition, besides a number of notes taken from living plants; to complete characters and correct some errors. I shall communicate to you all this as soon as I shall have time to assort my collections after my return to Honolulu.

In haste, yours most truly,

Wm. Hillebrand

---

[34] End of letter: "Dr. J. D. Hooker."
[35] Number in text is unclear; 3 feet seems correct.

Honolulu Sept. 24, 1870
Sir J. D. Hooker
My dear Sir,

  Your welcome favor of June 6 was handed to me on my return from the protracted excursion to the islands of Molokai, Lanai and Maui, about two weeks ago. I was also delighted to find in my yard that fine collection of Orchids which you have had the kindness to send me. Unfortunately they have been a much longer time on the way than I imagined they would have to be for the accompanying bill of delivery bears date May 28, while they have arrived on August 22. I fear that the Express Co. have sent the box by way of the isthmus on slow freight, which is so much less expensive to them, although their charges on arrival here $23.50 were high enough to cover the transit by the most expeditious route. As the consequence of the long voyage more than half of the plants had perished, out of 11 species only 5 being alive. I am really sorry that this experiment has not turned out more satisfactorily, so as to encourage us to follow up. In Maui I have visited the cinchona plantations on the south slope of Haleakala. There were about 500 plants in good condition, very rigorous, from 1–3 ft. high. They have not been planted high enough yet, their present position being at 2500–2800 ft. I requested Cpt. Makee to take up a number and plant them at 3500 ft. All these are suucirabra[?], no other kind having been raised that far.

  I am glad to hear that you have raised plants of Argyrosyphium. Let me tell you that this plant grows at the upper margin and inside the crater of Haleakala, between 8000 and 10,000 ft. on rocky ground. Rain is rather scant there, the cloud region being considerably lower. The temperature, although at night often very low 36–40F in winter the mountain cap has occasionally a short covering of snow, rises very high in the middle of the day, owing to the reflection of the sun rays from the steep rocks outside and from the high crater walls inside, probably to 82 or 84F. Abundant watering of the plts. will probably not bear[?]. From Lobelias I have sent you seeds of the magnificent Lobelia Gaudichandi and of the equally beautiful Hillebrandia Sandw. The former grows on the tabular summit of W. Maui near 7000 ft, on rather marshy grounds. The latter, on the whole, is one of the rarest plants of our islands. I found it in abundance in one of the deep and long mountain gorges of W. Maui, as almost to crowd out all other plants. It totally covered perpendicular rock-walls, cut[?] as they were, out of the core of the big mountain.

With the present I send another package of seeds—nearly 20 species, among them that splendid climber Strongylostra Cundium[?]. The result of this summer botanical excursion is very rich, comprising 7 new Lobeliaceae, among them one new Lobelia and two Clermontiae. You will have of all these within the next few months, with ample notes and remarks, but for the present the fine collection lies untouched in my study, for the astounding news from dear old fatherland fill my mind with to such a degree that there is no room for anything else beside it. I have done hardly anything but reading newspapers since my return. What a glorious rising of our people against that insolent foe! In future none of our neighbors will dare to interfere with the legitimate business of Germany to accomplish its union.

Day before yesterday I had the pleasure of becoming acquainted with that excellent man Sir George Grey, who on his way to New Zealand is spending a few days in Honolulu waiting for the Australian steamer. Yesterday he spent two hours in my garden in which he appeared to take an extraordinary interest. As he has been following in New Zealand about the same course, as I have been here for years, in the way of introducing valuable plants, I trust that a future correspondence and exchange will prove naturally advantageous.

By the last mail I had a letter from Mr. B. Roeze, the Belgian collector, who intends to visit the islands in a short time.

With my warmest thanks for the many favors received from you and hoping to receive often a few lines from your hand, I remain, dear Sir, with highest esteem,
Yours very truly
Wm Hillebrand

Puerto Orotavo February 22, 1881
Professor D. Oliver
Kew Gardens
Dear Sir,

Your letter of Nov. 27 and Dec. 3 were duly received and the package of Hawaiian Ponicea has also arrived some time ago. I confer myself to be under great obligation to Yourself and Mr. Bartham for the pains which you have taken with them. The appended notes and remarks by letter clear up nearly all those points of doubt, as which I expected to be enlightened by comparison with the plants in the Kew Herbarium, and the enclosed pikels[?] of 3 critical Beukey[?] species will enable me to give to these their proper positives.

May I now ask you to send me the manuscript as a registered package by mail? I have requested young Mr. Perez to enclose in this the postmarks to defray expense.

I do not know if I have to thank you or Sir Joseph Hooker for the Kew Gardens reports of the last year which I have read with great interest. In one of them I see the Pithorolobium Samang called the rain tree. I do not know in what country the tree enjoys such a reputation, but in the Sandwich Islands where it is a favorite tree for its magnificent size and large shady roof and where it is planted in nearly all settlements, nobody has ever suspected the tree to be endowed with such a precious gift.

The word "raintree" however reminds me of an observation which I made in April last in the island of Palma, on crossing the cumbre or coastal mountain range at an altitude of over 4000 ft. The eastern slope of the range is covered by a dense laurel forest which on the crest suddenly makes way to pines—pinus Canarius, growing, as usual, at considerable distances, but interspersed with brezos/Erica arborea/ and hayan/Myrian Yaga. The day was foggy and over the height of the cumber every ... and then quite a heavy fog cloud drifted along, but not a drop of rain fell on either slope, and the road was dusty as it had been all along since leaving the seashore. No sooner had I passed the divide and reached the roof of the first pine tree, when heavy drops fell over me and all around, as far as the branches extended, and no further, and the soil underneath was not only wet but converted in a regular quagmire. The hagar and brez... around all glistened with the water condensed on their leaves, as had done the laurels on the other side, but from none did it "rain." From the pines however it "rained" with heavy drops that I had to protect myself with the overcoat to examine a clump of [illegible]

which was growing at the foot of some of them. It is from that this phenomenon ceased about 400 ft below the crest, where the fog became lighter, but
the contrast of the pine with the other trees struck me greatly.

The explanation was not difficult to find. The long needles and
leaves of the tree which measure 8 inches and above and in their natural
position stretch out horizontally were all weighted downwards by the heavy
drops collected at their ends. As the drop fell, the liquid condensed as the
upper portions slid speedily with the moisture collected, and, by exposing
constantly a naked surface the temperature which became reduced below
that of the antricat by a slight evaporation caused by the wind, may have
tended to increase the precipitation bey[?] that which took place on neigh-
boring trees. On the broad horizontal leaf of the Naga the moisture
remained in situ and once formed to a certain thickness, would take away the
condition for further condensation. The needle leaves of the Erica however,
were too short to gather enough moisture and too stiff to yield to its weight.

Perhaps I am not telling you anything new and the same thing may
have been observed in Europe, but it seems to me that of all native or cul-
tures European pines the P. strobes is the only one which offers approaching-
ly [*sic*] similar conditions as to length and flexibility of leaves.

There would be no difficulty in conceiving, how a cluster of the
trees, or even a single one of large dimensions, if standing in a suitable locality, might feed a natural spring. Of course, I was reminded of the famous
"Garve," the "arbor mirabilis" of "The Island of Hierro," but on referring to
Vierar Dirivasio de Historie Natural de Cassolais Casarias, find has this
account possibly a pine, it probably was a Zibo or vinhatico, at all events a
Lamareau tree.

The island of Palma is much more abundantly supplied with water
than any other island of this group and at the same time is the one which still
holds pretty extensive pine forests. The people there maintain that the annual
rainfall is to small to account for the quantity of running water. It would be
difficult to prove the correctness of the opinion, but supposing it to be a fact,
it might not be unreasonable to make the pines account for that.

Dr. V. Perez, the father of young Dr. Perez, has raised several plants of
the Lotus peleirhyaikus which he proposes to deliver at Kew Gardens himself
next summer.

With my best regards yours very truly
W. Hillebrand

Heidelberg, Bergheimerstr. 18
March 30, [18]86
Dear Sir,[36]

Having just finished a Flora of the Hawaiian Islands I take the liberty to consult you on two points with reference to its publication. First, can I, without infringing on any ones right or privilege, copy in it their "Introduction or General Outlines of Botany" which forms a preface to the Flora of Hongkong and most other English Colonial Flowers? Or, if such right or privilege exists, would there be any difficulty in getting the permission granted to me on proper application?

Second, how many copies would it be safe to get printed? This may appear a queer question to you, but as I have no standard of comparison to go by, nor am I likely to obtain a reliable advice from German publishers — for the work is written in the English language, I should like to learn how many copies have been sold thus far of some English Colonial Flora of New Zealand, Benthams of Hongkong or Grisebach of the West Indies. Would You be kind enough to drop a line to the Publisher, Mss Lovell Reeve, and ask for the desired information? About 100 copies, I have been assure, could be disposed of to the Government and private parties in Honolulu and the Islands.

I shall be obliged, to undertake the publishing at my own expense, for the last Hawaiian Legislature refused the Government's proposal to aid me with a grant, to cover the expense of printing; but, as I indicated before, the Government may do something to assist me. The book will probably hold about 800 pages, but no plates, in it are described 993 species of phanerogams and Vascular Cryptogams among which about 100 new species.

Prolonged absence from Europe on account of my wife's illness, and since my return a protracted severe sickness of myself have caused annoying delays. Undoubtedly the work would have turned out better, if undertaken by one more competent than myself; but as no better one has stepped forward to do it, I trust that it will meet with good-natured indulgence. All I can say is that I have laboured honestly at it, and that my many years residence at the Islands and personal acquaintance with every one of them and their vegetation gives me a certain advantage over others who have to rely simply on herbarium specimens without knowing the country.

Would You also please to inform me, if Argyroxyphium Sandw., Cyanea superba, Hillebrandia Sandw., and some other rare plants of which

---

[36] End of letter: "Sir J. D. Hooker at Kew."

I sent seeds shortly before I left Honolulu in 1872, are growing at Kew?
        Trusting that You will favor me with a few lines at Your leisure, I
remain, dear Sir, with highest regards.
Your obedient servant
W. Hillebrand

P.S. May I ask You to favor me with the two last annual Reports of the
Kew Gardens?

Bibliography

I have investigated many sources; not all have been used. The following books, magazine articles, and reports I found particularly useful for my research and were used in compiling this book.

PRIMARY SOURCES
Documents:
Birth certificate of William Hillebrand.
Annual Report of the Theodorianische Gymnasium, 1839–1840.
Certificate of matriculation, Georg-August University, Goettingen.
Certificate of matriculation, Ruprecht-Karls University, Heidelberg.
Certificate of matriculation, curriculum vitae and dissertation, Humboldt University, Berlin.
31 copies of Hillebrand letters belonging to Kew Gardens, London, England.
One Hillebrand letter to Asa Gray, belonging to Harvard University.

SECONDARY SOURCES
Touring the River Murray. Royal Automobile Association of South Australia, 1986.

Bushnell, O. A. "Dr. Edward Arning, the First Microbiologist in Hawai'i." *Hawaiian Journal of History* 1 (1967).

Darragh, Thomas A., and Robert N. Wuchatsch. *From Hamburg to Hobsons Bay: German Emigration to Port Phillip (Australia Felix) 1848–51.* Melbourne: Thomas A. Darragh & Robert N. Wuchatsch – Wendish Heritage Society Australia, 1999.

Greer, Richard A. "Oahu's Ordeal: The Smallpox Epidemic of 1853." *Hawaii Historical Review: Selected Readings,* 1969.

Hackler, Rhoda E.A. Excerpts from *A History of Foster Park and Garden*, 1986.

Hillebrand, William. "Investigation of the Contagium of Leprosy." *The Pacific Commercial Advertiser*, February 3, 1883.

————. "The Relation of Forestry to Agriculture." *The Hawaiian Planters' Record* 22, 1920.

Kraehenbuehl, Darrell. "Pioneer German Botanists in Colonial South Australia, The Ones Who Stayed and Those Who Left." *The Naturalist* (Adelaide, South Australia), June 1998.

Struve, Walter. "Nineteen Century's German Melbourne on Display: Musings of a Curator." La Trobe University (Bundoora, Victoria, Australia), 2000.

INTERVIEWS
Five interviews with Jane Hillebrand Thompson.

BOOKS
The Hawaiian Journal of History. Volume 22 and 35. Honolulu: Hawaiian Historical Society, 1988.

Daws, Gavan. *Shoal of Time: A History of the Hawaiian Islands.* Honolulu: University of Hawai'i Press, 1968.

Day, A. Grove, ed. *Mark Twain's Letters from Hawaii.* Honolulu: University of Hawai'i Press, 1975.

Day, A. Grove, and Carl Stroven, eds. *A Hawaiian Reader.* Honolulu: Mutual Publishing.

De Varigny, Charles. *Fourteen Years in the Sandwich Islands, 1855–1868.* Honolulu: University of Hawai'i Press – Hawaiian Historical Society, 1981.

Dougherty, Michael. *To Steal A Kingdom: Probing Hawaiian History.* Honolulu: Island Style Press, 1992.

Fairchild, David. *The World Was My Garden: Travels of a Plant Explorer.* New York: Charles Scribner's Sons, 1938.

Joesting, Edward. *Hawaii: An Uncommon History.* New York: W.W. Norton & Co., 1972.

Krauss, Bob. *Grove Farm Plantation: The Biography of a Hawaiian Plantation.* Palo Alto, California: Pacific Books Publishers.

Kuykendall, Ralph S. *A History of the Hawaiian Kingdom.* 3 vols. Honolulu: University of Hawai'i Press, 1939–1967.

Lili'uokalani. *Hawaii's Story by Hawaii's Queen.* Rutland, Vermont: Charles E. Tuttle, 1964.

Musgrave, Toby, Chris Gardner, and Will Musgrave. *The Plant Hunters: Two Hundred Years of Adventure and Discovery Around the World.* London: Ward Lock, 1998.

Porteus, Stanley D. *Calabashes and Kings: An Introduction to Hawaii.* Rutland, Vermont: Charles E. Tuttle, 1970.

Schweizer, Niklaus R. *Turning Tide: The Ebb and Flow of Hawaiian Nationality.* New York: Peter Lang, 1999.

Soulé, Frank, John H. Gihon, and James Nisbet. *The Annals of San Francisco.* Berkeley, California: Berkeley Hills Books, 1998.

Whittle, Tyler. *The Plant Hunters: Tales of the Botanist-Explorers Who Enriched Our Gardens.* Philadelphia: Chilton Book Co., 1970.